NorthStar 1
LISTENING & SPEAKING

THIRD EDITION

Authors   **POLLY MERDINGER**

LAURIE BARTON

Series Editors   **FRANCES BOYD**

CAROL NUMRICH

Dedication

This book is dedicated to my husband Ricky, and our daughters Julia and Nina, who cannot remember a time in their lives when I was not writing *NorthStar*.

Polly Merdinger

I dedicate this book to my husband, Craig Binns, who took care of our children so that I could write.

Laurie Barton

NorthStar: Listening & Speaking Level 1, Third Edition

Copyright © 2015, 2009, 2003 by Pearson Education, Inc.
All rights reserved.

No part of this publication may be reproduced, stored in a retrieval system, or transmitted in any form or by any means, electronic, mechanical, photocopying, recording, or otherwise, without the prior permission of the publisher.

Pearson Education, 10 Bank Street, White Plains, NY 10606

Contributor credit: Natasha Haugnes

Staff credits: The people who made up the **NorthStar: Listening & Speaking Level 1, Third Edition** team, representing editorial, production, design, and manufacturing, are Kimberly Casey, Tracey Cataldo, Rosa Chapinal, Daniel Comstock, Aerin Csigay, Mindy DePalma, Dave Dickey, Graham Fisher, Nancy Flaggman, Niki Lee, Françoise Leffler, Amy McCormick, Mary Perrotta Rich, Robert Ruvo, Christopher Siley, Debbie Sistino, and Ken Volcjak.

Text composition: ElectraGraphics, Inc.
Editorial: Wildwood Ink

Library of Congress Cataloging-in-Publication Data

Barton, Laurie, authors.
  Northstar 1: Listening and speaking / Authors: Laurie Barton, Polly Merdinger. — Third Edition / Laurie Barton.
      pages cm
  Rev. ed. of: Northstar 1: listening and speaking, introductory / Polly Merdinger, Laurie Barton, 2008.
  ISBN-13: 978-0-13-338225-9
  ISBN-10: 0-13-338225-7
1. English language—Textbooks for foreign speakers. 2. English language—Spoken English—Problems, exercises, etc. 3. Listening—Problems, exercises, etc. I. Merdinger, Polly, authors. II. Title. III. Title: Northstar one. IV. Title: Listening and speaking.
  PE1128.M444 2015
  428.2'4—dc23
                                                                            2013050427

ISBN-10: 0-13-338225-7
ISBN-13: 978-0-13-338225-9

Printed in the United States of America
1 2 3 4 5 6 7 8 9 10—V057—20 19 18 17 16 15 14

CONTENTS

WELCOME TO

NORTHSTAR

A BLENDED-LEARNING COURSE FOR THE 21ST CENTURY

Building on the success of previous editions, *NorthStar* continues to engage and motivate students through new and updated contemporary, authentic topics in a seamless integration of print and online content. Students will achieve their academic as well as language and personal goals in order to meet the challenges of the 21st century.

New for the THIRD EDITION

★ Fully Blended MyEnglishLab

NorthStar aims to prepare students for academic success and digital literacy with its fully blended online lab. The innovative new MyEnglishLab: *NorthStar* gives learners immediate feedback—anytime, anywhere—as they complete auto-graded language activities online.

★ NEW and UPDATED THEMES

Current and thought-provoking topics presented in a variety of genres promote intellectual stimulation. The authentic content engages students, links them to language use outside of the classroom, and encourages personal expression and critical thinking.

★ EXPLICIT SKILL INSTRUCTION and PRACTICE

Language skills are highlighted in each unit, providing students with systematic and multiple exposures to language forms and structures in a variety of contexts. Concise presentations and targeted practice in print and online prepare students for academic success.

★ LEARNING OUTCOMES and ASSESSMENT

A variety of assessment tools, including online diagnostic, formative and summative assessments, and a flexible gradebook, aligned with clearly identified unit learning outcomes, allow teachers to individualize instruction and track student progress.

THE NORTHSTAR APPROACH TO CRITICAL THINKING

What is critical thinking?

Most textbooks include interesting questions for students to discuss and tasks for students to engage in to develop language skills. And often these questions and tasks are labeled critical thinking. Look at this question as an example:

When you buy fruits and vegetables, do you usually look for the cheapest price? Explain.

The question may inspire a lively discussion with students exploring a variety of viewpoints—but it doesn't necessarily develop critical thinking, Now look at another example:

When people in your neighborhood buy fruits and vegetables, what factors are the most important: the price, the freshness, locally grown, organic (without chemicals)? Make a prediction and explain. How can you find out if your prediction is correct? This question does develop critical thinking. It asks students to make predictions, formulate a hypothesis, and draw a conclusion—all higher-level critical thinking skills. Critical thinking, as philosophers and psychologists suggest, is a sharpening and a broadening of the mind. A critical thinker engages in true problem solving, connects information in novel ways, and challenges assumptions. A critical thinker is a skillful, responsible thinker who is open-minded and has the ability to evaluate information based on evidence. Ultimately, through this process of critical thinking, students are better able to decide what to think, what to say, or what to do.

How do we teach critical thinking?

It is not enough to teach "about" critical thinking. Teaching the theory of critical thinking will not produce critical thinkers. Additionally, it is not enough to simply expose students to good examples of critical thinking without explanation or explicit practice and hope our students will learn by imitation.

Students need to engage in specially designed exercises that aim to improve critical-thinking skills. This approach practices skills both implicitly and explicitly and is embedded in thought-provoking content. Some strategies include:

- subject matter that is carefully selected and exploited so that students learn new concepts and encounter new perspectives.
- students identifying their own assumptions about the world and later challenging them.
- activities that are designed in a way that students answer questions and complete language-learning tasks that may not have black-and-white answers. (Finding THE answer is often less valuable than the process by which answers are derived.)
- activities that engage students in logical thinking, where they support their reasoning and resolve differences with their peers.

Infused throughout each unit of each book, *NorthStar* uses the principles and strategies outlined above, including:

- Make Inferences: inference comprehension questions in every unit
- Vocabulary and Comprehension: categorization activities
- Vocabulary and Synthesize: relationship analyses (analogies); comparisons (Venn diagrams)
- Synthesize: synthesis of information from two texts teaches a "multiplicity" approach rather than a "duality" approach to learning; ideas that seem to be in opposition on the surface may actually intersect and reinforce each other
- Focus on the Topic and Preview: identifying assumptions, recognizing attitudes and values, and then re-evaluating them
- Focus on Writing/Speaking: reasoning and argumentation
- Unit Project: judgment; choosing factual, unbiased information for research projects
- Focus on Writing/Speaking and Express Opinions: decision-making; proposing solutions

THE NORTHSTAR UNIT

1 FOCUS ON THE TOPIC

* **CT** Each unit begins with a photo that draws students into the topic. Focus questions motivate students and encourage them to make personal connections. Students make inferences about and predict the content of the unit.

MyEnglishLab

CT A short self-assessment based on each unit's learning outcomes helps students check what they know and allows teachers to target instruction.

*indicates Critical Thinking

2 FOCUS ON LISTENING

Two contrasting, thought-provoking listening selections, from a variety of authentic genres, stimulate students intellectually.

VOCABULARY

1 🎧 Read and listen to the information about how Mia Pearlman makes sculptures. Mia uses paper to make very big sculptures. You can see them in many museums and galleries all over the world.

FREQUENTLY ASKED QUESTIONS ABOUT MIA PEARLMAN'S PAPER ART

How does Mia Pearlman make her sculptures?

Mia is very different from other artists. She makes her art in a very **unusual** way. First, Mia goes to the museum or gallery, and she looks at the **space**. She needs to know: "How big is the space? Does it have any windows? Does it have any sunlight?" This is important because Mia makes each sculpture for one **specific** space.

COMPREHENSION

Gee's Bend is the name of a very small town in Alabama. The women of Gee's Bend are famous for their quilts.

🎧 Listen to the documentary about the women from Gee's Bend. Choose the best way to complete each sentence.

1. The women in Gee's Bend make quilts _____.

   a. because they are artists

   b. to use on their beds

CT Students predict content, verify their predictions, and follow up with a variety of tasks that ensure comprehension.

🎧 Listen to these excerpts and fill in the missing main ideas and details. Remember to listen for general words and specific words.

Main Ideas	Details
Excerpt One The quilts are unusual.	_____
Excerpt Two They make their quilts with material from old clothes.	_____
Excerpt Three _____	One woman's great-grandmother said, "Let me tell you my story. Listen to the story of my life."

■■■■■■■■■■■■■■■■■■■■■■■■■■ GO TO MyEnglishLab FOR MORE SKILL PRACTICE.

CONNECTING THE LISTENINGS

STEP 1: Organize

Who can say these sentences? Write **Yes** or **No** under Mia Pearlman, A Woman from Gee's Bend, or both. Some answers have been done for you.

	MIA PEARLMAN	A WOMAN FROM GEE'S BEND
I am an artist.	Yes	No
I make sculptures.	Yes	No
I use unusual materials.	Yes	
I use expensive materials.		No
I put together many pieces.		
I always make a plan before I begin.		
My work has many colors.	No	
I work alone.		No
I make my art for one specific space.		No
My work is in museums.		
My work has a special meaning.		
My work lasts a long time.		Yes

40 UNIT 2

CT Students are challenged to take what they have learned and organize, integrate, and synthesize the information in a meaningful way.

1 Unit 2

Vocabulary Practice

Drag and drop the words to the correct places.

| nature | draw | specific | control | unusual | last | sculptures | cut | material | parts | space |

1. Mia Pearlman uses paper to make beautiful _____
2. Mia's art is very different from traditional art. Her art is _____
3. Many people think that paper is not a good _____ for sculptures.
4. They say this because paper isn't very strong. It doesn't _____ a long time.
5. Each sculpture is very big, so Mia needs to put it in a very big _____
6. Mia doesn't have a _____ plan when she makes a new sculpture.
7. To start, she uses a black pen to _____ many lines on the paper.
8. Then, she uses scissors to _____ the paper
9. She cuts out all the white _____ of the paper, and she takes them to the museum.
10. Mia's art looks like clouds and wind because she loves _____
11. Her art shows that nature is strong, and people cannot _____ it.

ALWAYS LEARNING   PEARSON

MyEnglishLab

Auto-graded vocabulary practice activities reinforce meaning and pronunciation.

EXPLICIT SKILL INSTRUCTION AND PRACTICE

MAKE INFERENCES

UNDERSTANDING SURPRISING STATEMENTS

An inference is a guess about something that is not directly stated. To make an inference, use information that you understand from what you hear.

Sometimes a speaker says something that is surprising to the listener. The speaker may tell the listener unusual *information*, or may use *a word* in a new or unusual way. In these situations, we have to make an inference to understand why the listener feels surprised.

Here are some phrases we use to express surprise:

Really?   Interesting!   That's (a little/very) unusual.   I don't understand!

🎧 Listen to an excerpt from the interview. Choose the best answer to question 1. In question 2, circle **a** or **b** to explain why the information is surprising.

Example

1. Why is the writer surprised?

   Mia (*played with Barbie dolls / made "Barbie worlds"*) when she was very young.

   The correct answer is: Mia made "Barbie worlds" when she was very young.

   Explanation

   Many little girls play with Barbie dolls, so that is **not** surprising.

   Most girls make up stories about their dolls' lives. But when Mia played with dolls, she *didn't make up stories about their lives.* She wanted *to make the world where the dolls lived.*

2. This **is** surprising because the museum guide _____.

   a. tells unusual information

   b. uses a word in a new or unusual way

   The correct answer is: **a.**

   Explanation

   a. Most children think only about their lives and about their family and friends. They don't think about the world. **This is unusual.**

CT Step-by-step instructions and practice guide students to exercise critical thinking and to dig deeper by asking questions that move beyond the literal meaning of the text.

LISTENING SKILL

IDENTIFYING MAIN IDEAS AND DETAILS

When you listen to a story or report, it's important to separate main ideas and details. Of course, the main ideas are very important. Why are **details** important?

Details can:

- help you to understand the main idea.
- highlight the main idea—show why it is important.
- give you a good example so you can remember the main idea.
- add "color" or beautiful language that you might enjoy.

🎧 Listen carefully to the vocabulary that the speaker uses. The main ideas have **general** vocabulary. The details have **specific** vocabulary.

Example

MAIN IDEA	DETAIL
These women work just like **artists**.	They decide how to put all the pieces together, always in new and different ways.

Artists is a general word. (There are many kinds of artists.) How do *these specific* artists work?

The detail explains this. It gives us two examples:

They decide how to put all the pieces together, always in new and different ways.

(continued on next page)

Making Unusual Art   39

Explicit skill presentation and practice lead to student mastery and success in an academic environment.

MyEnglishLab

Key listening skills are reinforced and practiced in new contexts. Meaningful and instant feedback provides students and teachers with essential information to monitor progress.

Using models from the unit listening selections, the pronunciation and speaking skill sections expose students to the sounds and patterns of English as well as to functional language that prepares them to express ideas on a higher level.

PRONUNCIATION

FINAL INTONATION

At the end of a sentence, we use special *intonation*. This means that our voice may go up to a higher pitch or note ("rising" intonation), or it may go up and then down ("rising-falling" intonation).

When you:

a. make a **statement**

OR

b. ask a *wh-* question ("information question")

your voice **rises** (*goes up*) on the last stressed syllable, and then it **goes down** to a low sound.

Wh- question words include:

who, what, where, when, why, how, how much/many

To ask a *yes/no* question, your voice rises (*goes up*) on the last stressed word or after the last stressed syllable.

STATEMENTS:

(one-syllable word)

I only wanted to make the *place* where Barbie **LIved**.

(two-syllable word)

Mia is an unusual **PERson**.

Wh- QUESTIONS:

(one-syllable word)

What do you **MEan**?

(two-syllable word)

What's going to happen to this **SCULPture**?

Yes / No QUESTIONS:

(one-syllable word)

Is that why her sculptures are so **BIG**?

(two-syllable word)

Do you see that **WINdow**?

1 🎧 Listen to the intonation at the end of these sentences. Does the speaker's voice go "up" or "up-down" on the last stressed word (marked in **bold**)? Circle the correct answer.

a. Mia's sculptures look like things we see in **nature**. (*up / up-down*)

b. What's going to **happen**? (*up / up-down*)

c. Is it going to a different **museum**? (*up / up-down*)

4 Compare your arrows with your partner's and the teacher's. Then practice reading the conversation aloud with your partner. Pay special attention to use correct intonation.

SPEAKING SKILL

EXPRESSING OPINIONS

When we say our opinion, we often begin with a phrase such as "I think." Here are some other useful phrases:

In my opinion, . . .   I believe (that) . . .

If you ask me, . . .   I feel (that) . . .

I feel (that) Mia Pearlman's art is beautiful.

In my opinion, the Gee's Bend women are true artists.

If you ask me, eggshell sculpture is not real art.

I believe (that) art is a good way to express your ideas about the world.

Work with a partner. Student A: Tell Student B your opinion about the type of art in number 1. Begin with one of the phrases from the box. You can also add a sentence to say if you like it or not. Then ask Student B, "What do **you** think?" Student B: Explain your opinion. Begin with one of the phrases from the box. Then switch roles.

Example *Mia Pearlman's art*

STUDENT A: **In my opinion**, *Mia Pearlman's paper art is beautiful. I love it.*
                 (opinion)   (like/dislike)

    What do **you** think?

STUDENT B: **I feel that** *it's very unusual. I like it a lot.*
               (opinion)   (like/dislike)

1. modern art

    A: **If you ask me,** _____

      What do you think?

    B: _____

(continued on next page)

MyEnglishLab

Students continue online practice of key pronunciation and speaking skills with immediate feedback and scoring.

MyEnglishLab

Home | Help | Test student, reallylongname@emailaddress.com | Sign out

NORTHSTAR 1   LISTENING & SPEAKING

1   Unit 2

Speaking Skill: Final Intonation

Read each sentence. Is the intonation rising or rising-falling? Drag and drop the sentences to the correct categories.

Move

Do you feel the same way?   Why do you like this painting?   Does it have a special meaning?
Do you like this kind of art?   Is this your favorite kind of art?   If you ask me, this art is very unusual.
In my opinion, it's very difficult to make this.   Why do you feel that way?   I can take it or leave it.
Why is this art interesting?   Is it difficult to make this kind of art?   Why is this a good piece of art for a museum?
I believe that people want to see art that is different.   Do you like this sculpture?   Is this art interesting?

Rising intonation:	Rising-falling intonation:
Do you feel the same way? *(Example)*	Why do you like this painting? *(Example)*

ALWAYS LEARNING

PEARSON

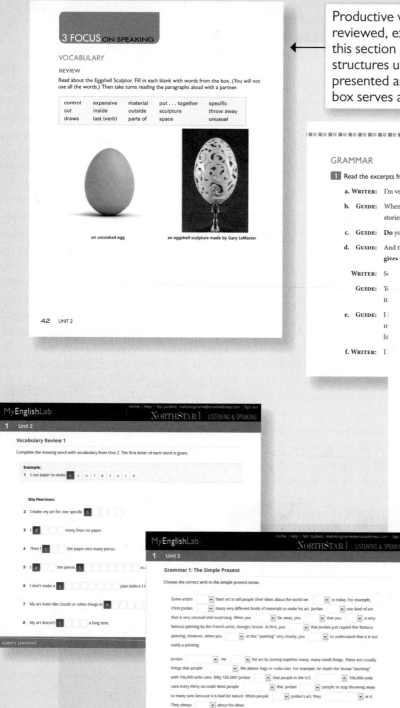

Productive vocabulary targeted in the unit is reviewed, expanded upon, and used creatively in this section and in the final speaking task. Grammar structures useful for the final speaking task are presented and practiced. A concise grammar skills box serves as an excellent reference.

3 FOCUS ON SPEAKING

VOCABULARY

REVIEW

Read about the Eggshell Sculptor. Fill in each blank with words from the box. (You will not use all the words.) Then take turns reading the paragraphs aloud with a partner.

control	expensive	material	put . . . together	specific
cut	inside	outside	sculpture	throw away
draws	last (verb)	parts of	space	unusual

an uncooked egg

an eggshell sculpture made by Gary LeMaster

42 UNIT 2

■■■■■■■■■■■■■■■■■■■■■■■■■■■ GO TO MyEnglishLab FOR MORE VOCABULARY PRACTICE.

GRAMMAR

1 Read the excerpts from the interview. Notice the verbs in **bold**.

a. **WRITER:** I'm very interested in Mia Pearlman's art.

b. **GUIDE:** When little girls **play** with dolls, like Barbie dolls, they usually **make up** stories about them.

c. **GUIDE:** **Do** you **see** that window?

d. **GUIDE:** And the sunlight from outside *really* **comes** through the window. . . . It **gives** the sculpture light.

WRITER: S

GUIDE: Y
it

e. **GUIDE:** I
m
li

f. **WRITER:** I

Look at the sentences on page 45.

1. Underline all the forms of the verbs *be* and *have*.

2. Look at all the other verbs.

   a. Which verbs end with s?

   b. Why?

   c. After the subjects *I, You,* and *They*, the verb (ends with **s** / doesn't end with **s**).

THE SIMPLE PRESENT	
1. Use the simple present tense for everyday actions or facts.	Mia Pearlman **makes** sculptures. The Gee's Bend women **make** quilts.
2. When the subject is the third-person singular—*he, she,* or *it*: put an *s* at the end of the main verb.	Paper **moves** and **changes**. (= It)
NOTE: After the subjects: *everything, something, nothing, anything everybody, somebody, nobody, anybody* use the third-person singular (*s* form).	*Everything* in the world **changes**.
NOTE: The verbs *be* and *have* are irregular.	*be: am, is, are* (See Unit 1.) *have:* I **have** some questions. The writer **has** some questions.
3. To form negative statements with contractions, use: *doesn't* or *don't* + the base form of the verb.	Paper **doesn't last** forever. The women in Gee's Bend **don't have** a plan for their quilts.
4. For *yes/no* questions, use: *Do* (or *Does*) + subject + the base form of the verb.	**Do** you **see** the window?
5. For *wh-* questions, use: *Wh-* word + *do* (or *does*) + subject + the base form of the verb.	Why does Mia Pearlman **use** paper?

6 UNIT 2

MyEnglishLab

Home | Help | Test student, reallylongname@emailaddress.com | Sign out

NORTHSTAR 1   LISTENING & SPEAKING

1   Unit 2

Vocabulary Review 1

Complete the missing word with vocabulary from Unit 2. The first letter of each word is given.

Example:

1 I use paper to make a [s][c][u][l][p][t][u][r][e].

Mia Pearlman:

2 I make my art for one specific [s].

3 I [d] many lines on paper.

4 Then I [c] the paper into many pieces.

5 I [p] the pieces t in a

6 I don't make a [s] plan before I b

7 My art looks like clouds or other things in [n].

8 My art doesn't [l] a long time.

ALWAYS LEARNING

MyEnglishLab

Home | Help | Test student, reallylongname@emailaddress.com | Sign out

NORTHSTAR 1   LISTENING & SPEAKING

1   Unit 2

Grammar 1: The Simple Present

Choose the correct verb in the simple present tense.

Some artists [ ] their art to tell people their ideas about the world we [ ] in today. For example, Chris Jordan [ ] many very different kinds of materials to make his art. Jordan [ ] one kind of art that is very unusual and surprising. When you [ ] far away, you [ ] that you [ ] a very famous painting by the French artist, Georges Seurat. At first, you [ ] that Jordan just copied this famous painting. However, when you [ ] at this "painting" very closely, you [ ] to understand that it is not really a painting.

Jordan [ ] He [ ] his art by putting together many, many small things. These are usually things that people [ ] like plastic bags or soda cans. For example, he made the Seurat "painting" with 106,000 soda cans. Why 106,000? Jordan [ ] that people in the U.S. [ ] 106,000 soda cans every thirty seconds! Most people [ ] this. Jordan [ ] people to stop throwing away so many cans because it is bad for nature. When people [ ] Jordan's art, they [ ] at it. They always [ ] about his ideas.

Submit

ALWAYS LEARNING   PEARSON

MyEnglishLab

Auto-graded vocabulary and grammar practice activities with feedback reinforce meaning, form, and function.

CT A final speaking task gives students an opportunity to exchange ideas and express opinions in sustained speaking contexts using vocabulary, grammar, pronunciation, listening, and speaking skills presented in the unit.

4. Mia Pearlman's sculpture *Inrush*

A: **I believe** _____

   What do you think?

B: _____

▪▪ ▪▪ ▪▪ ▪▪ ▪▪ ▪▪ ▪▪ GO TO **My**English**Lab** FOR MORE SKILL PRACTICE AND TO CHECK WHAT YOU LEARNED.

FINAL SPEAKING TASK

A role play is a short performance. The students take on roles, or become characters, and act out a situation.
You are going to role-play a discussion about what kind of art to buy for a museum. Use the vocabulary, grammar, intonation, and phrases for expressing opinions from this unit.*

Role-play: Choosing Unusual Art for a Modern Art Museum.

You work for a Modern Art Museum. The Museum wants to buy one new piece of art. You are going to choose the art.

STEP 1: Meet in three groups:

   Group 1: Mia Pearlman's paper sculpture

   Group 2: a Gee's Bend quilt

   Group 3: an eggshell sculpture

_____
* For Alternative Speaking Topics, see page 55.

In each group, look carefully at the picture(s) of your art and discuss these questions:

a. Is this art beautiful or interesting?

b. Is it difficult to make this art?

c. Does this art have a special meaning? What is it?

d. Did the artist use unusual material?

e. How will people feel when they see this art?

f. Why is this art important or special?

g. Why is this a good piece of art for a modern art museum?

STEP 2: Now, form new groups of three. Each new group has one person from each "art" group.

You and your partners work for the same modern art museum. You need to decide which type of art to buy for your museum. You can buy only one piece of art. Take turns speaking about the art you discussed in Step 1. Tell your partners why that art is the best one to buy. If anyone says, "That is not art," explain why it *is* art.

Listeners: Ask questions about the art your partners are describing.

STEP 3: Decide together which type of art you are going to buy for your museum.

STEP 4: Compare your answers with the other groups.

_____

Group 1: Mia Pearlman's paper sculpture

"Eddy," * a paper sculpture by Mia Pearlman

hat moves in a circle

UNIT PROJECT

STEP 1: Work with a partner. Do research online about *traditional paper art* from one of these countries (or any other country that you are interested in):

China, Germany, India, Indonesia, Japan, Korea, Mexico, Poland, Turkey

STEP 2: Print some pictures or be prepared to show some online images of the type of art you researched.

STEP 3: Together with your partner, prepare to speak to your class for 3 minutes about what you learned. Don't memorize a speech. Just practice speaking about the type of paper art you researched.

Practice pronouncing the key words in your presentation before you speak. Ask your teacher to help you with this *before* your presentation.

STEP 4: Take turns speaking and presenting your pictures/photos to your classmates. Be sure to make eye contact with all of your classmates as you speak. Answer any questions that your classmates ask you.

Listening Task

Listen to your classmates' presentations. Ask them a question about something you don't understand completely, or ask them to give you more information

ALTERNATIVE SPEAKING TOPICS

1. Does your country have a traditional type of art (paper or other type)? What materials do people use to make it?

2. In your country, do students take art classes in school?

   a. If yes: At what age? (elementary school, junior high school, high school) Do the students *make* art, *learn about* art, or *study* famous art?

   b. If no: Is this OK? Why or why not?

   c. Is it important to have art classes in school? Why or why not?

3. Do you have any art in your room, apartment, or house? What kind of art is it? (paintings, posters, sculptures) What kind of art do you like to have in your home?

▪▪ ▪▪ ▪▪ ▪▪ ▪▪ ▪▪ ▪▪ GO TO **My**English**Lab** TO DISCUSS ONE OF THE ALTERNATIVE TOPICS, WATCH A VIDEO ABOUT ART, AND TAKE THE UNIT 2 ACHIEVEMENT TEST. ▪▪ ▪▪ ▪▪ ▪▪ ▪▪ ▪▪ ▪▪

CT A group unit project inspires students to inquire further and prepares students to engage in real-world activities. Unit projects incorporate Internet research, helping to build students' digital literacy skills.

INNOVATIVE TEACHING TOOLS

With instant access to a wide range of online content and diagnostic tools, teachers can customize learning environments to meet the needs of every student.

USING MyEnglishLab, NORTHSTAR TEACHERS CAN:

Deliver rich online content to engage and motivate students, including:

- student audio to support listening and speaking skills.
- engaging, authentic video clips, including reports adapted from ABC, NBC, and CBS newscasts, tied to the unit themes.
- opportunities for written and recorded reactions to be submitted by students.

Use a powerful selection of diagnostic reports to:

- view student scores by unit, skill, and activity.
- monitor student progress on any activity or test as often as needed.
- analyze class data to determine steps for remediation and support.

Use Teacher Resource eText* to access:

- a digital copy of the student book for whole class instruction.
- downloadable achievement and placement tests.
- printable resources including lesson planners, videoscripts, and video activities.
- classroom audio.
- unit teaching notes and answer keys.

---

* Teacher Resource eText is accessible through MyEnglishLab: *NorthStar*

STUDENT BOOK and MyEnglishLab

★ Student Book with MyEnglishLab

The two strands, Reading & Writing and Listening & Speaking, for each of the five levels, provide a fully blended approach with the seamless integration of print and online content. Students use MyEnglishLab to access additional practice online, view videos, listen to audio selections, and receive instant feedback on their work.

eTEXT and MyEnglishLab

★ eText with MyEnglishLab

Offering maximum flexibility for different learning styles and needs, a digital version of the student book can be used on iPad® and Android® devices.

★ Instructor Access: Teacher Resource eText and MyEnglishLab (Listening & Speaking 1–5)

Teacher Resource eText

Each level and strand of *NorthStar* has an accompanying Teacher Resource eText that includes: a digital student book, unit teaching notes, answer keys, downloadable achievement tests, classroom audio, lesson planners, video activities, videoscripts, and a downloadable placement test.

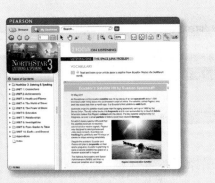

MyEnglishLab

Teachers assign MyEnglishLab activities to reinforce the skills students learn in class and monitor progress through an online gradebook. The automatically-graded exercises in MyEnglishLab *NorthStar* support and build on academic skills and vocabulary presented and practiced in the Student Book/eText. The teacher-graded activities include pronunciation, speaking, and writing, and are assigned by the instructor.

★ Classroom Audio CD

The Listening & Speaking audio contains the recordings and activities, as well as audio for the achievement tests. The Reading & Writing strand contains the readings on audio.

SCOPE AND SEQUENCE

UNIT OUTCOMES	1 FRIENDSHIP **A WORLD OF FRIENDS** pages 2–27 *Listening 1: The Friendship Force* *Listening 2: The Best Summer of My Life*	2 ART **MAKING UNUSUAL ART** pages 28–55 *Listening 1: Mia Pearlman* *Listening 2: The Quilts of Gee's Bend*
LISTENING	• Make and confirm predictions • Identify main ideas and details • Recognize and use *and* and *but* to introduce similar and contrasting ideas MyEnglishLab Vocabulary and Listening Skill Practice	• Make and confirm predictions • Identify and distinguish between main ideas and details • Recognize phrases that express surprise MyEnglishLab Vocabulary and Listening Skill Practice
SPEAKING	• Express opinions • Ask for more information • Describe someone's personality **Task:** Introduce a friend MyEnglishLab Speaking Skill Practice and Speaking Task	• Express opinions • Express likes and dislikes **Task:** Create and dramatize a group discussion MyEnglishLab Speaking Skill Practice and Speaking Task
INFERENCE	• Infer a speaker's reaction	• Infer meaning from statements that express surprise
PRONUNCIATION	• Recognize common rhythm patters • Pronounce stressed and unstressed words in sentences MyEnglishLab Pronunciation Skill Practice	• Recognize and pronounce rising and rising-falling intonation at the end of statements and questions MyEnglishLab Pronunciation Skill Practice
VOCABULARY	• Infer word meaning from context MyEnglishLab Vocabulary Practice	• Infer word meaning from context MyEnglishLab Vocabulary Practice
GRAMMAR	• Recognize and use the present and past tenses of the verb *be* MyEnglishLab Grammar Practice	• Recognize and use the simple present tense MyEnglishLab Grammar Practice
VIDEO	MyEnglishLab *Fans Forever—The Beatles*, ABC News, Video Activity	MyEnglishLab *Fish Artist*, ABC News, Video Activity
ASSESSMENTS	MyEnglishLab Check What You Know, Checkpoints 1 and 2, Unit 1 Achievement Test	MyEnglishLab Check What You Know, Checkpoints 1 and 2, Unit 2 Achievement Test

3 SPECIAL POSSESSIONS
SPECIAL POSSESSIONS
pages 56–81
Listening 1: The Story of Dream Catchers
Listening 2: Toys in College

4 BUSINESS
CREATIVITY IN BUSINESS
pages 82–109
Listening 1: KK Gregory, Young and Creative
Listening 2: A Business Class

• Make and confirm predictions • Identify main ideas and details • Order statements based on ideas in a listening selection • Recognize speech markers that show excitement MyEnglishLab Vocabulary and Listening Skill Practice	• Make and confirm predictions • Identify main ideas and details • Recognize signal words for main ideas in a lecture MyEnglishLab Vocabulary and Listening Skill Practice
• Express agreement and disagreement • Support ideas with reasons • Ask questions to include others in a conversation **Task:** Discuss, describe, and report on special possessions MyEnglishLab Speaking Skill Practice and Speaking Task	• Express opinions • React to general and surprising information **Task:** Create and dramatize a business meeting MyEnglishLab Speaking Skill Practice and Speaking Task
• Infer a speaker's beliefs	• Infer contrasting ideas by noticing stress
• Distinguish between the three -s endings of present tense verbs MyEnglishLab Pronunciation Skill Practice	• Recognize and pronounce the *th* sounds MyEnglishLab Pronunciation Skill Practice
• Infer word meaning from context MyEnglishLab Vocabulary Practice	• Infer word meaning from context MyEnglishLab Vocabulary Practice
• Recognize and use adverbs of frequency in the simple present tense MyEnglishLab Grammar Practice	• Recognize and use *there + be* in the present and past tense MyEnglishLab Grammar Practice
MyEnglishLab *Wedding Dress Crisis Averted,* ABC News, Video Activity	MyEnglishLab *Hawking Hot Dogs,* ABC News, Video Activity
MyEnglishLab Check What You Know, Checkpoints 1 and 2, Unit 3 Achievement Test	MyEnglishLab Check What You Know, Checkpoints 1 and 2, Unit 4 Achievement Test

SCOPE AND SEQUENCE

UNIT OUTCOMES	5 PHOBIAS UNDERSTANDING FEARS AND PHOBIAS pages 110–133 *Listening 1: Psyched: A Radio Show* *Listening 2: Crossing a Bridge*	6 ADVENTURE RISKS AND CHALLENGES pages 134–161 *Listening 1: The Amazing Swimmer, Diana Nyad* *Listening 2: An Outward Bound Experience*
LISTENING	• Make and confirm predictions • Identify main ideas and details • Recognize and understand meaning behind contradictions MyEnglishLab Vocabulary and Listening Skill Practice	• Make and confirm predictions • Identify main ideas and details • Recognize the use of *even though* to express an unexpected or surprising result MyEnglishLab Vocabulary and Listening Skill Practice
SPEAKING	• Express opinions • Give advice using imperative verbs **Task:** Create and dramatize a situation about phobias MyEnglishLab Speaking Skill Practice and Speaking Task	• Express opinions • Express an unexpected or surprising result using *even though* • Compare and contrast information from two listenings **Task:** Create and dramatize an interview with a risk-taker MyEnglishLab Speaking Skill Practice and Speaking Task
INFERENCE	• Infer meaning from exaggerations	• Infer meaning from rhetorical questions
PRONUNCIATION	• Recognize and pronounce the three *-ed* endings in the regular past tense MyEnglishLab Pronunciation Skill Practice	• Recognize and pronounce words with the vowel sounds /iy/ and /ɪ/ MyEnglishLab Pronunciation Skill Practice
VOCABULARY	• Infer word meaning from context MyEnglishLab Vocabulary Practice	• Infer word meaning from context • Recognize and use adjectives ending in *-ing* and *-ed* MyEnglishLab Vocabulary Practice
GRAMMAR	• Recognize and use the simple past tense with regular and irregular verbs MyEnglishLab Grammar Practice	• Recognize and use the present continuous tense MyEnglishLab Grammar Practice
VIDEO	MyEnglishLab *Unusual Phobias*, Healthguru, Video Activity	MyEnglishLab *Cockpit Cool*, ABC News, Video Activity
ASSESSMENTS	MyEnglishLab Check What You Know, Checkpoints 1 and 2, Unit 5 Achievement Test	MyEnglishLab Check What You Know, Checkpoints 1 and 2, Unit 6 Achievement Test

7 FAMILY
ONLY CHILD—LONELY CHILD?
pages 162–189

Listening 1: Changing Families
Listening 2: How Do Only Kids Feel?

- Make and confirm predictions
- Identify main ideas and details
- Take notes using a graphic organizer
- Identify advantages and disadvantages

MyEnglishLab Vocabulary and Listening Skill Practice

- Express opinions
- Express agreement, disagreement, and uncertainty

Task: Create and dramatize a conversation between parents

MyEnglishLab Speaking Skill Practice and Speaking Task

- Infer meaning based on word choice

- Recognize and understand the appropriate use of *going to* vs. *gonna*

MyEnglishLab Pronunciation Skill Practice

- Infer word meaning from context

MyEnglishLab Vocabulary Practice

- Recognize and use the future tense with *be going to*

MyEnglishLab Grammar Practice

MyEnglishLab *You and Your Siblings*, ABC News, Video Activity

MyEnglishLab Check What You Know, Checkpoints 1 and 2, Unit 7 Achievement Test

8 SPORTS
SOCCER: THE BEAUTIFUL GAME
pages 190–216

Listening 1: The Sports File
Listening 2: America Talks

- Make and confirm predictions
- Identify main ideas and details
- Recognize signal words that introduce reasons and results (*because, because of, so, that's why*)
- Categorize information from two listenings

MyEnglishLab Vocabulary and Listening Skill Practice

- Express and support opinions with reasons
- Express and explain reasons and results

Task: Create and present a TV commercial

MyEnglishLab Speaking Skill Practice and Speaking Task

- Infer meaning from comparisons with *be like*

- Recognize the use of contrastive stress

MyEnglishLab Pronunciation Skill Practice

- Infer word meaning from context

MyEnglishLab Vocabulary Practice

- Recognize and make comparisons with regular and common irregular adjectives

MyEnglishLab Grammar Practice

MyEnglishLab *Game On*, ABC News, Video Activity

MyEnglishLab Check What You Know, Checkpoints 1 and 2, Unit 8 Achievement Test

ACKNOWLEDGMENTS

Many people contributed to this book at various stages of its development, and I would like to acknowledge all of them. First, the *NorthStar* series exists because of the creative vision of Frances Boyd and Carol Numrich. I am very grateful to them for inviting me to contribute to this series.

Frances Boyd edited the original manuscript of all three editions and offered ideas and support throughout the writing process. I thank her for all of her valuable contributions to this text. Debbie Sistino, the Editorial Manager of the *NorthStar* series, is the editor that every author dreams of. She guided this book from original manuscript to publication of all three editions with incredible dedication, talent, professionalism, and most importantly, good humor. I am extremely grateful for the trust she has always shown in the classroom teacher's expertise and experience. For guiding this text through its third edition I am extremely grateful to my development editor, Mary Perrotta Rich. Mary made many valuable editorial contributions, and was unfailingly patient and supportive, even under the pressure of very tight deadlines. I am also very grateful to editor Tamera Bryant, whose support and great sense of humor helped to guide this book through its final stages, and whose suggestions greatly enhanced the final product. Thanks also to Aerin Csigay for his work in procuring the photographs used in the text.

For her invaluable work in developing the online component of this text—MyEnglishLab—I wish to thank Niki Lee. I am very grateful to Niki for her instruction in creating online materials, as well as her patience and support as I went through the learning process to create this important part of the *NorthStar* series. Great thanks also to Andrea Bryant, who joined this project midstream and helped to bring it to its completion.

To my wonderful colleagues at Columbia University's American Language Program, from whom I have been learning for over 30 years: Thank you for making my professional journey so challenging, so rewarding, and so much fun! You have all enriched my life immeasurably.

Finally, and most importantly, for so generously allowing me to share their life stories, I am grateful beyond words to Mia Pearlman, Gary LeMaster, KK Gregory, Nancy L., and Jeremy Merdinger. My great thanks too to Jillian Walters of Friendship Force International for sharing information about this wonderful organization.

—Polly Merdinger

I would like to thank my husband Craig Binns. This book could not have been written without his love and support.

—Laurie Barton

REVIEWERS

Chris Antonellis, Boston University – CELOP; Gail August, Hostos; Aegina Barnes, York College; Kim Bayer, Hunter College; Mine Bellikli, Atilim University; Allison Blechman, Embassy CES; Paul Blomquist, Kaplan; Helena Botros, FLS; James Branchick, FLS; Chris Bruffee, Embassy CES; Nese Cakli, Duzce University; María Cordani Tourinho Dantas, Colégio Rainha De Paz; Jason Davis, ASC English; Lindsay Donigan, Fullerton College; Bina Dugan, BCCC; Sibel Ece Izmir, Atilim University; Érica Ferrer, Universidad del Norte; María Irma Gallegos Peláez, Universidad del Valle de México; Jeff Gano, ASA College; María Genovev a Chávez Bazán, Universidad del Valle de México; Juan Garcia, FLS; Heidi Gramlich, The New England School of English; Phillip Grayson, Kaplan; Rebecca Gross, The New England School of English; Rick Guadiana, FLS; Sebnem Guzel, Tobb University; Esra Hatipoglu, Ufuk University; Brian Henry, FLS; Josephine Horna, BCCC; Arthur Hui, Fullerton College; Zoe Isaacson, Hunter College; Kathy Johnson, Fullerton College; Marcelo Juica, Urban College of Boston; Tom Justice, North Shore Community College; Lisa Karakas, Berkeley College; Eva Kopernacki, Embassy CES; Drew Larimore, Kaplan; Heidi Lieb, BCCC; Patricia Martins, Ibeu; Cecilia Mora Espejo, Universidad del Valle de México; Kate Nyhan, The New England School of English; Julie Oni, FLS; Willard Osman, The New England School of English; Olga Pagieva, ASA College; Manish Patel, FLS; Paige Poole, Universidad del Norte; Claudia Rebello, Ibeu; Lourdes Rey, Universidad del Norte; Michelle Reynolds, FLS International Boston Commons; Mary Ritter, NYU; Minerva Santos, Hostos; Sezer Sarioz, Saint Benoit PLS; Ebru Sinar, Tobb University; Beth Soll, NYU (Columbia); Christopher Stobart, Universidad del Norte; Guliz Uludag, Ufuk University; Debra Un, NYU; Hilal Unlusu, Saint Benoit PLS; María del Carmen Viruega Trejo, Universidad del Valle de México; Reda Vural, Atilim University; Douglas Waters, Universidad del Norte; Leyla Yucklik, Duzce University; Jorge Zepeda Porras, Universidad del Valle de México

A WORLD OF
Friends

1 FOCUS ON THE TOPIC

1. Read the title of the unit. What does it mean?

2. Look at the photo. Are the people friends or family? Where are they?

3. Do you have friends from other countries? How did you meet them?

GO TO MyEnglish**Lab** *TO CHECK WHAT YOU KNOW.*

2 FOCUS ON LISTENING

VOCABULARY

 Look at the list of countries. Is there a Friendship Force club in your country?

A Friendship Force visitor from the U.S. with her host family in Norway

Friendship Force Member Countries

Australia	Costa Rica	India	Nepal	Slovakia
Austria	Croatia	Indonesia	Netherlands	South Africa
Azerbaijan	Cyprus	Israel	New Caledonia	Sweden
Belarus	Czech Republic	Italy	New Zealand	Taiwan (ROC)
Belgium	Egypt	Japan	Norway	Tanzania
Bosnia and Herzegovina	Estonia	Jordan	Peru	Thailand
Brazil	France	Kenya	Philippines	Turkey
Burundi	Georgia	Korea	Poland	Ukraine
Canada	Germany	Latvia	Romania	United Kingdom
Cayman Islands	Ghana	Mexico	Russia	United States
Chile	Hungary	Mongolia	Singapore	Vietnam
Colombia				

2 🎧 Read and listen to the radio commercial for the Friendship Force.

"A World of Friends Is a World of Peace[1]"

And now, a message from the Friendship Force. The Friendship Force says, "A world of friends is a world of peace."

The Friendship Force is an **international** friendship organization.[2] Friendship Force groups **travel** to **foreign** countries. In the new country, the Friendship Force visitors **stay** with **host families**. They learn about their host family's life and **culture**. The visitors and their host families **spend** a lot of **time** together and they become good friends.

Every year, Friendship Force visitors **make** 40,000 new **friends** in 56 different countries. This is important because when people make international friends, they help to make peace in the world.

Are you **interested in** the Friendship Force? Please go to our website for more information. If you want to travel with the Friendship Force, send us an **application** so we can learn more about you. And remember, "a world of friends is a world of peace."

---

[1] **peace:** good relationships; the opposite of war/fighting
[2] **organization:** a large group or company

3 Circle the correct answer to complete the sentence.

The Friendship Force says, "When you have friends in foreign countries, _____."

a. you help to bring peace to the world   **b.** you can be in the Friendship Force

4 Match the boldfaced words on the left with the definitions on the right. Write the letter of the correct definition on the line.

_____ 1. The Friendship Force goes to 56 different countries. It is an **international** organization.

_____ 2. Friendship Force visitors **travel** to many different countries.

_____ 3. Friendship Force visitors want to learn about **foreign** countries.

_____ 4. Friendship Force visitors **stay** in a family's home.

_____ 5. Friendship Force visitors stay with a **host family** in a foreign country.

_____ 6. The visitors and their host families do many things together. They **spend time** together every day.

_____ 7. Host families teach their visitors about their **culture**; for example, their holidays and food.

_____ 8. Friendship Force visitors like to **make friends** with people in different countries.

_____ 9. I like to read books about Japan and talk to Japanese people. I **am interested in** Japan.

_____ 10. Write all your information on your **application** to the Friendship Force: your name, address, e-mail, and phone number.

a. get to know new people

b. a page with information about yourself

c. do things

d. not your country or language

e. go on a trip; go to a different place

f. from many different countries

g. live in a place for a short time

h. customs

i. like to learn about

j. a family that invites a foreign visitor to live with them for some time.

GO TO MyEnglishLab FOR MORE VOCABULARY PRACTICE.

PREVIEW

Nina and Rick are talking about the Friendship Force. Listen to the beginning of the conversation. Then answer the questions.

1. What are you listening to? Check (✓) the answer.

_____ a telephone call   _____ a radio talk show

2. What will Nina and Rick talk about? Check (✓) your ideas.

_____ host families   _____ shopping   _____ traveling

_____ hotels   _____ music   _____ groups

_____ students   _____ children   ✓ languages

MAIN IDEAS

1 🎧 Listen to the whole conversation. Look again at questions 1 and 2 in the Preview on pages 6–7. Were any of your answers correct? Did they help you to understand the conversation?

2 🎧 Listen again. Read the sentences. Write **T** (true) or **F** (false). Correct the false information.

_____ **1.** Friendship Force visitors can be young or old.

_____ **2.** Some Friendship Force visitors stay in hotels.

_____ **3.** Nina wants to stay with a host family in Thailand.

_____ **4.** All host families speak English.

_____ **5.** Nina and Rick think it's good to have international friends.

DETAILS

🎧 Listen again. Circle the correct answer to complete each sentence.

1. Friendship Force groups have _____ people.

   a. 13 to 50   **b.** 15 to 30

2. Friendship Force groups meet for the first time _____.

   a. before they travel   **b.** in the foreign country

3. Nina thinks, "When you live with a host family, you learn _____."

   a. their language   **b.** about their country

(continued on next page)

4. Nina _____ Thai (the language of Thailand).

    a. speaks a little   **b.** doesn't speak

5. Friendship Force visitors stay with their host family for one or two _____.

    a. weeks   **b.** months

6. After they stay with their host family, many Friendship Force visitors travel _____.

    a. to a different country   **b.** in the same country

GO TO MyEnglishLab FOR MORE LISTENING PRACTICE.

MAKE INFERENCES

MAKING INFERENCES BASED ON REACTIONS

An **inference** is a guess about something that is not directly stated. To make an inference, use information that you understand from what you hear.

In a conversation, people often express a positive (good) or negative (bad) **reaction**. They tell *how they feel about* the other person's idea. **When we understand people's reactions,** it's easier to make inferences about them and their feelings.

🎧 Listen to the example. What is Nina's reaction?

Example

QUESTION   **NINA:** Well, first, can college students be in the Friendship Force?

ANSWER   **RICK:** Sure. We have people of all ages—teenagers, college students, even grandparents!

REACTION   **NINA:** **Oh, that's great.**

1. Nina has a (*positive / negative*) reaction.

2. She _____.

    a. is probably a college student   **b.** probably knows some college students

The correct answers are: 1. positive, 2. **a.**

Explanation

Reaction: Nina asks, "Can college students be in the Friendship Force?" Rick's answer means "yes." Nina's **reaction** is, **"Oh, that's great."** This shows that Nina has a *positive* feeling about Rick's answer. She is happy about it.

Inference: Why is Nina happy?
Nina has a positive reaction, so we can *infer* that she is probably a college student, and she wants to travel with the Friendship Force.

Listen to the excerpts from the conversation and think about the speaker's reaction. Then make an inference about the speaker's feeling. Circle the correct answer to complete each sentence.

Excerpt One

1. Nina has a (*positive* / *negative*) reaction.

2. Nina is not worried about living with a host family, so she is probably a _____ person.

   a. shy   **b.** friendly

Excerpt Two

1. Nina has a (*positive* / *negative*) reaction.

2. Nina is worried because she doesn't speak Thai. She is really asking Rick, "Will I _____?"

   a. have problems with my host family   **b.** learn the language

Excerpt Three

1. Nina has a (*positive* / *negative*) reaction.

2. Nina likes the idea of "people, not places." She thinks you can learn more about a foreign country when you _____.

   a. meet the people   **b.** visit the important places

EXPRESS OPINIONS

Discuss the questions with the class.

1. Do you think it's good to stay with a host family? Why or why not?

2. Do you need to speak the same language well to make friends with someone? Why or why not?

3. What are the best ways to learn about another country?

■ ■ ■ ■ ■ ■ ■ ■ ■ ■ ■ ■ ■ ■ ■ ■ ■ *GO TO* MyEnglishLab *TO GIVE YOUR OPINION ABOUT ANOTHER QUESTION.*

COMPREHENSION

Students help to plant a garden in Costa Rica.

Annie Quinn is an American high school student. Last summer, she traveled to Costa Rica with a group called The Experiment in International Living (EIL).

🎧 **Listen to the interview with Annie. Circle the correct information to complete each sentence.**

1. The students in Annie's group came from different (*states / countries*).

2. Some of the students (*spoke different languages / had different religions*).

3. The students in Annie's group stayed in Costa Rica for (*a month / two weeks*).

4. Annie loved the students in her group and (*Ana / her host family*).

5. Annie's host family (*was very friendly / had a daughter*).

6. Annie learned Spanish in her Spanish class and from her (*host family / Spanish friends*).

7. Annie learned that speaking the same language is not always (*a good idea / necessary*).

8. Experiment groups usually stay in a foreign country for (*two / three to five*) weeks.

9. *Experiment* groups go to (*27* / *37*) different countries.

10. *Experiment* students (*can take different kinds of classes / always take language classes*).

VOCABULARY

Fill in the blanks with the vocabulary from the box. Read the conversation with a partner. Then switch roles and read it again.

anything else	at first	became	have problems + (____ing)	warm

Annie is talking on the phone with her good friend Cory in Philadelphia.

CORY: So—how is Costa Rica? Are you having a good time?

ANNIE: Well, _____ I didn't know anyone, so I was a little nervous.
1.

CORY: Sure . . .

ANNIE: But now I love it here. Everyone in my group is so _____. We all
2.
_____ good friends very quickly!
3.

CORY: That's wonderful.

ANNIE: I know. I'm very lucky.

CORY: And how is your host family? Do you _____ speaking with them in
4.
Spanish?

ANNIE: No, I don't. They're so nice, and they're helping me to learn a lot.

CORY: Great! And how is your Spanish class?

ANNIE: Oh, it's very good. I really like my teacher.

CORY: That's good! Do you have any other classes?

ANNIE: No way! I have my Spanish class every morning, and then I speak Spanish all day
with my host family. I don't have time to study _____.
5.

CORY: That makes sense.

GO TO MyEnglishLab *FOR MORE VOCABULARY PRACTICE.*

LISTENING SKILL

PREDICTING INFORMATION AFTER *AND* AND *BUT*

Noticing how people use *and* and *but* can help you to understand their meaning.

We use *and* to connect two sentences with **similar kinds of** information. The information can be: two good things, two problems, two similar things, two differences, etc.

We use *but* to connect two sentences with **contrasting** (or opposite) information. The information can be: one good thing/one bad thing (problem), one similarity/one difference, etc.

🎧 Listen to the examples.

Examples

A. Annie: "... we all came from different states, **and** we had different religions and
          (a difference)   (a difference)

cultures."

Annie uses *and* because the first sentence tells about *a difference*, and the second sentence *also* tells about a *difference*. In other words, the second sentence adds more information that is **similar** to the information in the first sentence.

B. Annie: "At first, I didn't speak much Spanish, **but** I learned a lot of Spanish from them
          (negative information)   (positive information)

and in my Spanish class, too."

Annie uses *but* because the first sentence has *negative* information and the second sentence has *positive* information. In other words, the information in the second sentence is **contrasting (opposite)**.

🎧 Listen to the excerpts from Annie's interview. You will hear the first sentence and the word **and** or **but**. Try to predict what kind of information the second part of the sentence will have. Circle the sentence ending that makes sense. Then listen to the complete sentence to check your answer.

Excerpt One

a. I loved my host family.

b. I had some problems with my host family.

Excerpt Two

a. We all came from the same states.

b. We all came from different states.

Excerpt Three

a. At first, I spoke Spanish well.

b. At first, I didn't speak much Spanish.

GO TO MyEnglishLab *FOR MORE SKILL PRACTICE.*

CONNECT THE LISTENINGS

STEP 1: Organize

Think about the information in Listening One and Listening Two. Check (✓) the correct column(s) for each sentence. You may check both columns.

	FRIENDSHIP FORCE	EXPERIMENT IN INTERNATIONAL LIVING
1. Visitors know each other before they travel.	✓	
2. People of any age can be in the group.		
3. Only high school students can be in the group.		✓
4. You can go with the group only in the summer.		
5. The visitors stay with host families.		
6. The visitors stay with host families for three, four, or five weeks.		
7. There are many classes.		✓
8. It's not necessary to speak the host family's language.		
9. The host families do not always speak English.	✓	✓
10. Applications are on the website.		

STEP 2: Synthesize

Judy is a 15-year-old student. She is studying Chinese. She wants to visit China so she can practice speaking Chinese. Judy is talking to her friend Mei about different groups.

Role-play with a partner. Complete the conversation with information from Step 1: Organize. Add five more lines for Judy and for Mei.

JUDY: The Friendship Force and The Experiment in International Living are both great! How can I decide?

MEI: Well, let's see. In the Friendship Force, you meet everyone before you travel. Everyone is from the same city.

JUDY: That's nice, but it's not so important. I like meeting new people from different cities.

MEI: OK. Experiment is only for . . .

JUDY: The Friendship Force . . .

MEI: . . .

JUDY: . . .

GO TO MyEnglishLab TO CHECK WHAT YOU LEARNED.

3 FOCUS ON SPEAKING

VOCABULARY

REVIEW

A parent calls the American Field Service (AFS), an international student exchange program. Complete the conversation with the vocabulary from the box.

anything else	have problems + (-ing)	spend
application	host families	stay
become	international	traveling
culture	is interested in	warm
foreign	make friends	

AFS: Hello, AFS. Amanda Chu speaking.

PARENT: Hi, I'm calling for information about your _____ summer
_____1._____
programs for high school students.

AFS: Yes, how can I help you?

PARENT: Well, my son wants to _____ the summer in a
_____2._____
_____ country.
_____3._____

AFS: Great. Do you know what country he _____?
_____4._____

PARENT: Well, he speaks a little Spanish. Can he go to a country in South America?

AFS: Sure. We have three groups that are _____ to Argentina this
_____5._____
summer.

PARENT: Oh, that's great. Can you tell me a little about the program? What do the
students do?

AFS: Well, first, the students all go to Buenos Aires, the capital city, for one week.
They study Spanish, and they learn about Argentine _____.
_____6._____

PARENT: That's a good idea.

AFS: Yes, and it also gives them time to _____ with each other,
_____7._____
before they go to their Argentine _____.
_____8._____

PARENT: How long do they _____ with their host families?
_____9._____

AFS: They live with them for a month. And most students say it's the best time of
their lives.

PARENT: Do all the host families speak English?

AFS: Most of them speak a little English. But the students and the host families
never _____ understanding each other. The host families are
_____10._____
always very _____ and friendly people. The students and the
_____11._____
families always _____ good friends.
_____12._____

(continued on next page)

PARENT: This sounds like a great program for my son. Can you e-mail me the

_____?
13.

AFS: Sure! I'll send it right now. Do you need to know _____?
14.

PARENT: No, I don't think so. Thanks so much for your help.

EXPAND

1 Read the conversation and the adjectives in the box. The adjectives describe people's personalities. Each word is listed with its opposite.

QUESTION: What's he like? / What's she like?
This means: "What kind of personality does he/she have?"
Or: "How can you describe him/her?"

ANSWER: He's/She's (adjective).

friendly/warm	talkative	serious	quiet
funny	calm	boring	nervous
interesting	nice/kind	lazy	mean
hardworking	shy		

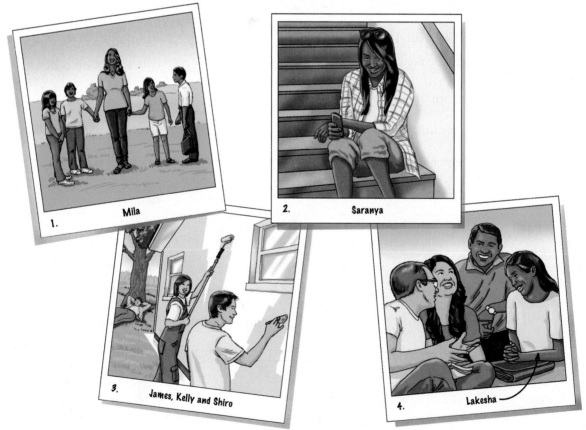

1. Mila

2. Saranya

3. James, Kelly and Shiro

4. Lakesha

16   UNIT 1

2 Annie is showing her parents pictures of her friends from her summer in Costa Rica. She is telling her parents about each person. Work with a partner. Look at the pictures. For each picture, complete the conversation using adjectives from the box. Take turns.

Use this model:

PARENT: Who's that?

ANNIE: That's _____ *Mila* _____.

PARENT: What's she/he like?

ANNIE: She's/He's _____ *friendly* _____.

CREATE

1 Complete the first column with information **about yourself.**

a. What are you like? Write three adjectives.

b. Then write your answers to the questions:

- Do you like to travel or spend time at home?
- What are you interested in?
- What do you have problems doing?

2 Interview two classmates. Ask them the same questions. Write their answers in the chart.

YOU	CLASSMATE A: _____	CLASSMATE B: _____
I am: _____ _____ _____	_____ is: _____ _____ _____	_____ is: _____ _____ _____
I like to (travel)/ spend time at home). I am interested in _____. I have problems _____. (verb) -ing	_____ likes to (travel / spend time at home). _____ is interested in _____. _____ has problems _____. (verb)-ing	_____ likes to (travel / spend time at home). _____ is interested in _____. _____ has problems _____. (verb)-ing

3 Share your answers with the class. Tell about one classmate who is **similar to you** and one who is **different from you**.

Example

SIMILAR: Kei and I are quiet.

DIFFERENT: I like to travel, but Sam likes to spend time at home.

GO TO MyEnglishLab *FOR MORE VOCABULARY PRACTICE.*

GRAMMAR

1 Read the excerpts. Follow the directions.

NINA: My name is Nina Rodriguez, and I'm interested in the Friendship Force.

RICK: Language isn't so important.

ANNIE: My group was great! We were all American high school students.

   If you're in high school and you want to have a great summer, go on The Experiment in International Living!

1. Underline all the present forms of *be*. Circle all the past forms of *be*.

2. What **negative** forms of *be* can you find? _____

PRESENT AND PAST TENSE OF *BE*

1. The present tense of *be* has three forms:

am	I **am** Nina.
is	She **is** my friend. / He **is** my friend.
are	It **is** a friendship organization.
	You **are** my friend.
	We **are** friends. / They **are** friends.

To form negative statements, use:

am	I **am not** Nina.
is + *not*	He **is not** my friend.
are	She **is not** my friend.
	They **are not** friends.

2. Contractions are short forms. Use affirmative and negative contractions in speaking and in informal writing.	**I'm** Nina.	**I'm not** from Costa Rica.
	You're my friend.	**You're not** my . . .
	He's my friend.	**He's not** . . .
	She's my friend.	**She's not** . . .
	It's a friendship organization.	**It's not** a . . .
	We're friends.	**We're not** . . .
	They're friends.	**They're not** . . .
Another way to form negative statements with contractions is:		
subject + (**be** + **n't**)	(This form does not work with *I*.)	
	You aren't from Costa Rica.	
	He/She isn't . . .	
	It isn't . . .	
	We aren't . . .	
	They aren't . . .	
3. The past tense of **be** has two forms:	I	
was	You	
	He / She / It **was** here yesterday.	
were	We **were** here yesterday.	
	They	
4. To form negative statements in the past tense, use:	I **was not (wasn't)** in class yesterday.	
was / were + **not**	They **were not (weren't)** in class yesterday.	
or the contractions		
wasn't / weren't		
5. To form questions in the present and the past tense, use:	**Is she** your friend?	
Question word + **be** + **subject**	**Are you** friends now?	
	Where is your friend now?	
	When were you in Costa Rica?	

2 Complete the conversation with the correct form of *be*. Use contractions wherever possible. Then check your answers with a partner's. Read the conversation together.

> **friendship force**
> INTERNATIONAL
>
> ### Friendship Force International
>
> ### Changing the Way You See the World
>
> 127 PEACHTREE ST NW • SUITE 501 • ATLANTA, GA 30303 USA • PH 404.522.9490

Q: What kind of people does the Friendship Force look for?

A: Friendship Force visitors _____*are*_____ interested in other cultures. They
                                                    1.
_____ afraid of new places.
        2. (neg.)

Q: _____ it necessary to speak another language?
            3.

A: No, it _____! Language _____ a big problem for the
                    4. (neg.)   5. (neg.)
visitors.

Q: What if we have a problem when we _____ in another country?
                                                        6.

A: Every Friendship Force group has a leader. The leader _____ always
                                                                        7.
near you. For example, last year, one visitor _____ sick in Germany.
                                                            8.
Her host family called her Friendship Force leader. The leader took her to the
doctor immediately. Luckily, she _____ very sick. The next day, she
                                            9. (neg.)
_____ fine. So remember, when you travel with the Friendship Force,
        10.
you _____ alone.
        11. (neg.)

Q: I really want to travel with the Friendship Force, but I _____ sure
                                                                        12. (neg.)
when I can go. _____ that a problem?
                        13.

A: No, that _____ a problem. There _____ many different
                    14. (neg.)   15.
groups every year. The schedule _____ on our website.
                                            16.

▪▪▪▪▪▪▪▪▪▪▪▪▪▪▪▪▪▪▪▪▪▪▪▪▪▪▪▪▪▪ GO TO MyEnglishLab FOR MORE GRAMMAR PRACTICE.

PRONUNCIATION

RHYTHM: STRESSED AND UNSTRESSED WORDS

Listen to the short conversation.

A: WHERE are you **FROM**?

B: I'm from **CHI**na. HOW about **YOU**?

A: COsta RIca.

These sentences show the rhythm of English sentences. The words and syllables in CAPITAL letters are STRESSED. They are **longer** and **louder** than the other words and syllables. They also have a **higher pitch** or sound.

The last word in each sentence is **STRESSED MORE** than the other stressed words. It is the longest, loudest, and highest pitch word. The last word usually tells the most important information.

Words that are usually STRESSED:	Words that are usually NOT stressed:
nouns and proper nouns (names)	pronouns
main verbs	the verbs *be* and *have*
negative verbs	auxiliary verbs (*do, does*)
adjectives	articles (*a, an, the*)
adverbs	prepositions (*to, from, in, on*)
question words	
demonstratives (*this, that*)	

1 The rhythm at the beginning of each group of sentences shows the rhythm of all the sentences in the group. Listen to the sentences and repeat them.

1. Rhythm: DA da da **DA**

    a. WHERE are you **FROM**?

    b. HOW about **YOU**?

    c. THIS is my **FRIEND**.

    d. KEI'S from Ja**PAN**.

    e. WHAT do you **DO**?

(continued on next page)

2. Rhythm: da da **DA** da

    a. He's from **CHI**na.

    b. I'm a **STU**dent.

    c. Is she **FRIEND**ly?

    d. It's ex**CI**ting.

    e. We have **HOME**work.

3. Rhythm: DA da **DA** da

    a. NICE to **MEET** you.

    b. THIS is **NI**na.

    c. WHAT'S the **PROB**lem?

    d. ANN'S a **STU**dent.

    e. WHAT's your **MA**jor?

4. Other rhythms:

a. da **DA**	I **KNOW**.	It's **GREAT**.	You're **RIGHT**.
b. da **DA** da	You're **WEL**come.	They're **DIFF**erent.	He's **FRIEND**ly.
c. da da **DA**	I'm in **CLASS**.	Okay, **GOOD**.	They were **GREAT**.

2 🎧 Listen to the conversation. Then practice it with a partner.

    LILY: **HI**. I'm **LI**ly.

  CARLOS: NICE to **MEET** you. I'm **CAR**los.

    LILY: WHERE are you **FROM**?

  CARLOS: I'm from **CO**sta **RI**ca. HOW about **YOU**?

    LILY: I'm from **CHI**na.

  CARLOS: WHAT do you **DO**?

    LILY: I'm a **STU**dent. HOW about **YOU**?

  CARLOS: I **WORK** in a **LAB**.

3 Work with a partner. Complete the conversation with the sentences from the box. Then practice the conversation with your partner.

> I'm from **TO**kyo. HOW about **YOU**?
> ~~NICE to **MEET** you. I'm **HI**ro.~~
> WHAT'S your **MA**jor?
> YES, I **AM**. HOW about **YOU**?
> THAT'S MY MAjor **TOO**!

YOON: Hi, I'm **YOON**.

HIRO: NICE to **MEET** you. I'm **HI**ro.

YOON: HI **HI**ro. WHERE are you **FROM**?

HIRO: _____

YOON: I'm from KOREA. Are you a **STU**dent?

HIRO: _____

YOON: I'm a **STU**dent, **TOO**.

HIRO: _____

YOON: MATH. HOW about **YOU**?

HIRO: _____

SPEAKING SKILL

ASKING FOR MORE INFORMATION

Sometimes in a conversation, we want to know more information.

Here are some useful ways to ask someone for more information:

NINA:	I'm interested in the Friendship Force, but **I have some questions**.
INTERVIEWER:	**Can you tell us about** your group?
	I'd like to know more about your host family.
ANNIE:	And I also learned that language is not always so important.
INTERVIEWER:	**What do you mean?**

Here are some useful phrases for asking for more information:

- I have a question / some questions.
- Can you tell (me / us) more about (it / that)?
- What do you mean?

- I'd like to know more about (that).
- Can I ask you a question?
- Why do you think so?

Work with a partner. Student A, read a statement. Student B, ask for more information. Student A, give Student B more information. Use the information from this unit or your own ideas.

> Example
>
> **A:** It's important for high school students to live in a foreign country.
>
> **B:** *Why do you think so?*
>
> **A:** It's the best way to learn about another country and to learn the language.

1. You can learn a lot when you travel.

2. With a friend, speaking the same language isn't really important.

3. The Experiment in International Living program is really great!

4. Friendship Force groups are very special.

Switch roles.

5. Living with a host family is a great experience.

6. It's very important to speak two languages.

7. Some people are really nervous when they go to a foreign country.

8. A world of friends is a world of peace.

■■■■■■■■■■■■GO TO MyEnglishLab FOR MORE SKILL PRACTICE AND TO CHECK WHAT YOU LEARNED.

FINAL SPEAKING TASK

In this activity, you are going to introduce one classmate to two other classmates. Try to use the vocabulary, grammar, pronunciation, and language for asking for information from this unit.*

Follow the steps.

STEP 1: Work with a partner. Student A, ask Student B questions about his or her profession or major/favorite subject in school, hobbies, native country or city, and native language. Take notes on your partner's answers. Then switch roles.

STEP 2: Find another pair of students (Students C and D).
Student A, tell the pair four things about Student B.
Students C and D, after each piece of information, ask Student B for more information. Use the phrases from the Speaking Skill on page 24.
Student B, answer the questions.

STEP 3: Complete the activity three more times, switching roles each time so that everyone in the group has a chance to tell about someone, ask for more information, and give more information.

Example

A: I'm going to tell you about my friend Francisco. He's new here.

C: **What do you mean?**

B: I moved here last week. I'm from Buenos Aires, Argentina.

A: Francisco speaks three languages.

D: That's so cool! **What languages do you speak?**

B: I speak Spanish, Portuguese, and some English.

C: Wow. **Can I ask you a question?**

B: Sure.

D: How did you learn Portuguese?

B: Well, I lived in Brazil for a year in high school. It's an amazing country.

D: **Why do you think so?**

B: Because I love soccer!

---

*For Alternative Speaking Topics, see page 27.

UNIT PROJECT

The Friendship Force works for world peace. Learn about another organization that works for world peace.

STEP 1: Choose an organization. You may choose from the following list.

- United States Peace Corps
- Médecins sans Frontières (Doctors without Borders)
- Seeds of Peace
- World Peace Project for Children
- Artists without Borders
- Kids without Borders
- Peace through the Arts Camp

STEP 2: Get information about the organization. Use the Internet or a library.

STEP 3: Give a report about the organization to a small group of your classmates.

Questions to Guide Your Research

1. What is the name of the organization?

2. Who can belong to the organization?

3. What does the organization do?

4. Where did the organization begin? When?

5. Would you like to work for this organization? Why or why not?

Listening Task

Listen to your classmates' reports. Write the name of each organization and ask each student two questions to get more information.

ALTERNATIVE SPEAKING TOPICS

Discuss one of the topics. Try to use the vocabulary, grammar, pronunciation, and language for asking for information from the unit.

1. Do groups like the Friendship Force, EIL, and AFS really help bring peace to the world? Why or why not?

2. Will there ever be peace in the world? Why or why not?

3. Did you ever live in another country? Tell about your experience there.

◾◾◾◾◾◾◾◾◾◾◾◾◾◾ GO TO MyEnglishLab TO DISCUSS ONE OF THE ALTERNATIVE TOPICS, WATCH A VIDEO ABOUT FRIENDSHIP, AND TAKE THE UNIT I ACHIEVEMENT TEST. ◾◾◾◾◾◾◾◾◾◾◾◾◾◾◾◾◾◾◾◾

MAKING UNUSUAL
Art

1 FOCUS ON THE TOPIC

1. Look at the photo. What kind of art is this? What material did the artist use?

2. What does the art look like? Do you like this art? Why or why not?

3. What kind of art do you like?

GO TO MyEnglishLab TO CHECK WHAT YOU KNOW.

LISTENING ONE MIA PEARLMAN

VOCABULARY

1 🎧 Read and listen to the information about how Mia Pearlman makes sculptures. Mia uses paper to make very big sculptures. You can see them in many museums and galleries all over the world.

FREQUENTLY ASKED QUESTIONS ABOUT MIA PEARLMAN'S PAPER ART

How does Mia Pearlman make her sculptures?

Mia is very different from other artists. She makes her art in a very **unusual** way. First, Mia goes to the museum or gallery, and she looks at the **space**. She needs to know: "How big is the space? Does it have any windows? Does it have any sunlight?" This is important because Mia makes each sculpture for one **specific** space.

Mia Pearlman standing in front of her sculpture, _Inrush_

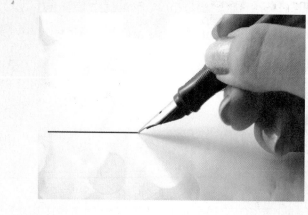

After Mia sees the space, she goes home and she starts to **draw**. She uses black ink and long pieces of white paper. She draws many different lines on the paper. She doesn't have a specific plan for these lines.

Then Mia **cuts** out all the white **parts of** the paper between the black lines. She usually cuts 30 to 80 pieces for each sculpture.

Mia goes back to the museum or gallery space. She puts all the pieces of paper on the floor. She thinks about how to make the sculpture. She doesn't have a plan. She decides her plan when she's in the space.

Finally, she puts all the pieces together to make the sculpture.

Paper isn't a very strong **material**. Why does Mia use paper for her sculptures?

Mia loves paper! She says paper is like everything in **nature**. She loves it because it always moves and changes, and it doesn't **last** forever.[1]

Why do many of Mia's sculptures look like clouds?[2]

Clouds are a beautiful part of nature, and people cannot **control** or change them. Mia's art helps people remember that nature is a very important part of the world.

---

[1] **forever:** for always; with no end

[2] **clouds:**

2 Take turns with a partner. Student A, read the sentence and choose the correct meaning of the word from the box. Student B, say, "Yes, I agree" or "No, I don't think so. I think . . . "

---

to make someone or something do what you want
x not common
x to make pictures with a pencil or pen
to stay in good condition
x something people use to make things
things that are not made by people (plants, animals, mountains, etc.)
special or exact
x to use scissors or a knife
x a place or area
~~art that you usually make with stone, metal, or clay~~
x a piece of the whole thing

Example

sculpture

A: A **sculpture** is *art that you usually make with stone, metal, or clay.*

B: Yes, I agree.

  1. A: A **space** is . . .
     B: (Yes . . . / No . . .)

  2. A: A **part of** something means . . .
     B: (Yes . . . / No . . .)

  3. A: **Specific** means . . .
     B: (Yes . . . / No . . . .)

  4. A: **Unusual** means . . .
     B: (Yes . . . / No . . .)

  5. A: To **draw** means . . .
     B: (Yes . . . / No . . .)

  6. A: **Material** is . . .
     B: (Yes . . . / No . . .)

7. **A:** To **cut** something means . . .

   B: (Yes . . . / No . . .)

8. **A:** **Nature** is . . .

   B: (Yes . . . / No . . .)

9. **A:** To **last** means . . .

   B: (Yes . . . / No . . .)

10. **A:** To **control** something means . . .

    B: (Yes . . . / No . . .)

GO TO MyEnglishLab FOR MORE VOCABULARY PRACTICE.

PREVIEW

Look at the photo and discuss these questions with the class:

What does this sculpture look like to you? What does it show? What will people think about when they see it?

MAIN IDEAS

1 🎧 A magazine writer is interviewing a museum guide about the artist, Mia Pearlman. Listen to the interview about Mia Pearlman. Look again at the questions in Preview. Were any of your answers correct? Did they help you to understand the interview?

2 🎧 Listen to the interview again. Choose the correct answer to complete each sentence.

1. Mia is interested in people and the _____ they live in.

    a. houses   **b.** world

2. Mia says people cannot _____ many things in the world.

    a. control   **b.** understand

3. Mia's art uses paper and _____.

    a. clouds   **b.** sunlight

4. Mia's art helps people to feel their connection to _____.

    a. nature   **b.** sculpture

5. Mia's sculptures teach people that everything in life _____.

    a. has an end   **b.** is beautiful

DETAILS

🎧 Read the sentences. Then listen to the interview again. Write **T** (true) or **F** (false). Correct the false information.

_____ **1.** Mia was interested in houses when she played with her dolls.

_____ **2.** Mia thinks that people are the most important part of the world.

_____ **3.** Some of Mia's sculptures are about the weather.

_____ **4.** The sculpture *Inrush* looks like it is moving.

_____ **5.** With *Inrush*, people can feel like they are inside a cloud.

_____ **6.** Mia's sculpture is similar to a play in a theater.

GO TO MyEnglishLab *FOR MORE LISTENING PRACTICE.*

MAKE INFERENCES

UNDERSTANDING SURPRISING STATEMENTS

An inference is a guess about something that is not directly stated. To make an inference, use information that you understand from what you hear.

Sometimes a speaker says something that is surprising to the listener. The speaker may tell the listener unusual *information*, or may use *a word* in a new or unusual way. In these situations, we have to make an inference to understand why the listener feels surprised.

Here are some phrases we use to express surprise:

Really?   *Interesting!*   *That's (a little/very) unusual.*   *I don't understand!*

🎧 Listen to an excerpt from the interview. Choose the best answer to question 1. In question 2, circle **a** or **b** to explain why the information is surprising.

Example

1. Why is the writer surprised?

Mia (*played with Barbie dolls / made "Barbie worlds"*) when she was very young.

The correct answer is: Mia made "Barbie worlds" when she was very young.

Explanation

Many little girls play with Barbie dolls, so that is **not** surprising.

Most girls make up stories about their dolls' lives. But when Mia played with dolls, she *didn't make up stories about their lives.* She wanted *to make the world where the dolls lived.*

2. This **is** surprising because the museum guide _____.

a. tells unusual information

b. uses a word in a new or unusual way

The correct answer is: **a.**

Explanation

a. Most children think only about their lives and about their family and friends. They don't think about the world. **This is unusual.**

(🎧) Listen to the excerpts from the interview. Choose the best answer to complete the sentence in number 1. Then circle **a** or **b** in number 2 to explain why the writer was surprised.

Excerpt One

1. Why is the writer surprised?

   She doesn't understand how a sculpture can (*end* / *go to a different museum*).

2. This is surprising because the museum guide:

   a. tells the writer unusual information.

   b. uses a word in a new or unusual way.

Excerpt Two

1. Why is the writer surprised?

   Mia doesn't want her sculptures to (*last for a long time* / *be in a museum*).

2. This is surprising because the museum guide:

   a. tells the writer unusual information.

   b. uses a word in a new or unusual way.

EXPRESS OPINIONS

Discuss the questions with the class.

1. When Mia Pearlman was a child, she understood that "the world is very big, and people are just a very small part of it." Did you ever have that feeling? How old were you? Where were you? Why did you feel that way?

2. Mia takes down her sculptures and never makes them again. Do you understand why she does this? Do you think it's OK or a bad idea? Why? What can you learn about Mia from this?

■■■■■■■■■■■■■■■■■■■■■■■■■■■GO TO MyEnglishLab TO GIVE YOUR OPINION ABOUT ANOTHER QUESTION.

COMPREHENSION

Gee's Bend is the name of a very small town in Alabama. The women of Gee's Bend are famous for their quilts.

🎧 Listen to the documentary about the women from Gee's Bend. Choose the best way to complete each sentence.

1. The women in Gee's Bend make quilts _____.

   a. because they are artists

   b. to use on their beds

2. The women make the quilts with _____.

   a. pieces of old clothes

   b. expensive material

3. The quilts are art because _____.

   a. they are beautiful and unusual

   b. they have so many pieces

(continued on next page)

4. One woman made a quilt to remember _____.

    a. her husband

    b. her mother

5. The quilts have a special meaning because _____.

    a. families make them together

    b. they have many colors

6. When they make the quilts, the older women tell the younger women _____.

    a. about their families

    b. about Africa

VOCABULARY

Work with a partner. Fill in the blanks with one of the words or phrases from the box. Then take turns reading the sentences aloud.

expensive	inside	outside	put . . . together	throw . . . away

How did the Gee's Bend quilts become famous? Here is the answer from one woman from Gee's Bend:

The women in Gee's Bend make a lot of quilts, so when the quilts get old, we don't keep

them. We just _____ them _____ and we make a new one.
                   1.

I had one very old quilt, so I took it _____ and I put it near the garbage. I didn't
                                               2.

want it.

And one day, a man named Bill Arnett came to Gee's Bend, and he saw my old quilt. And he

said, ."Look at that beautiful quilt!"

I thought he was crazy, and I said, "Here, you can have it." He asked me, "Do you have any

more quilts like this?"

So we went _____3._____ my house, and I showed him all my quilts. Bill paid me $2,000 for three of my·quilts!

Two thousand dollars?! How could my quilts be so _____4._____? I thought they were old and dirty, but Bill said they were art.

Then Bill bought a lot of quilts from different women in Gee's Bend, and he

_____5._____ them _____ in a museum! Can you believe that? It's true.

■■■■■■■■■■■■■■■■■■■■■■■■■■■■■■GO TO MyEnglishLab FOR MORE VOCABULARY PRACTICE.

LISTENING SKILL

IDENTIFYING MAIN IDEAS AND DETAILS

When you listen to a story or report, it's important to separate main ideas and details. Of course, the main ideas are very important. Why are **details** important?

Details can:

- help you to understand the main idea.
- highlight the main idea—show why it is important.
- give you a good example so you can remember the main idea.
- add "color" or beautiful language that you might enjoy.

  Listen carefully to the vocabulary that the speaker uses. The main ideas have **general** vocabulary. The details have **specific** vocabulary.

Example

MAIN IDEA	DETAIL
These women work just like **artists**.	They decide how to put all the pieces together, always in new and different ways.

Artists is a general word. (There are many kinds of artists.) How do *these specific* artists work?

The detail explains this. It gives us two examples:

They decide how to put all the pieces together, always in new and different ways.

(continued on next page)

🎧 Listen to these excerpts and fill in the missing main ideas and details. Remember to listen for general words and specific words.

Main Ideas	Details
Excerpt One	
The quilts are unusual.	Wh_____
	_____
Excerpt Two	
They make their quilts with material from old clothes.	likd_____
Excerpt Three	
_____	One woman's great-grandmother said, "Let me tell you my story. Listen to the story of my life."

■■■■■■■■■■■■■■■■■■■■■■■■■■■■■■■■■■■■ GO TO MyEnglishLab *FOR MORE SKILL PRACTICE.*

CONNECTING THE LISTENINGS

STEP 1: Organize

Who can say these sentences? Write **Yes** or **No** under Mia Pearlman, A Woman from Gee's Bend, or both. Some answers have been done for you.

	MIA PEARLMAN	A WOMAN FROM GEE'S BEND
I am an artist.	Yes	No
I make sculptures.	Yes	No
I use unusual materials.	Yes	
I use expensive materials.		No
I put together many pieces.		
I always make a plan before I begin.		
My work has many colors.	No	
I work alone.		No
I make my art for one specific space.		No
My work is in museums.		
My work has a special meaning.		
My work lasts a long time.		Yes

Mia Pearlman and a woman from Gee's Bend are speaking to a news reporter.

Role-play in groups of three. Complete the conversation with information from Step 1: Organize. Each speaker should add at least four more sentences to the conversation.

REPORTER:	Are you an artist?
GEE'S BEND WOMAN:	Oh no, I'm not really an artist.
REPORTER:	How about you?
MIA PEARLMAN:	Yes, I am an artist.
REPORTER:	What kind of art do you make?
GEE'S BEND WOMAN:	I make quilts.
MIA PEARLMAN:	And I make sculptures.
REPORTER:	Do you use any unusual materials?
GEE'S BEND WOMAN:	Well, I use old . . .
REPORTER:	And you?
MIA PEARLMAN:	Yes, I use . . .

GO TO MyEnglishLab TO CHECK WHAT YOU LEARNED.

VOCABULARY

REVIEW

Read about the Eggshell Sculptor. Fill in each blank with words from the box. (You will not use all the words.) Then take turns reading the paragraphs aloud with a partner.

control	expensive	material	put . . . together	specific
cut	inside	outside	sculpture	throw away
draws	last (verb)	parts of	space	~~unusual~~

an uncooked egg

an eggshell sculpture made by Gary LeMaster

The Eggshell Sculptor

Some artists today make art with very _____unusual_____ things, like old clothes,
1.

vegetables, old books, butterflies, and stones. Gary LeMaster makes beautiful art with a

different kind of unusual _____material_____. He uses eggshells! An eggshell is the hard
2.

_____special_____ part of an egg.
3.

How does he do it? First, he _____ a picture on the eggshell with a pencil.
4.

Then he uses a dentist's drill[3] to _____ out some small _____
5.   6.

the shell. Cutting the shell is very difficult. LeMaster needs to _____control_____ the
7.

drill very well. If he doesn't, the eggshell can break into many little pieces. Then he has to

_____cut_____ the eggshell and start again with a new one.
8.

When the _____ is finished, LeMaster puts a special material on it.
9.

Now the eggshell sculpture will not break. Then he puts each sculpture in a special

_____sculpture_____ so people can look at it, but not break it. Sometimes he puts his
10.

sculptures under glass. This way, the sculptures _____ a long time.
11.

LeMaster makes many different kinds of eggshell sculptures. Sometimes, people pay him to

make a _____ sculpture that they want. For example, one man asked LeMaster
12.

to make a sculpture of a football with his football team's name on it. Some of LeMaster's

sculptures are very _____expensive_____. People pay $2,000 or more for some of his very
13.

unusual eggshell sculptures.

_____

[3] **a dentist's drill:** a small machine that dentists use to make holes in teeth

EXPAND

1 Work with a partner. Read the expressions. Then write them on the scale from 0 to 5. (**0** is for a very negative opinion, and **5** is for a very positive opinion.)

It's my favorite (kind of art).	I like it.
I don't like it (at all).	(It's OK, but) I'm not crazy about it.
~~I love it.~~	I like it a lot.
~~I hate it.~~	I like it very much.
I can take it or leave it.	

5: *I love it.* _____   _____

4: _____   _____

3: _____   _____

2: _____

1: _____

0: *I hate it.* _____

2 Share your answers with the class.

3 Practice the expressions. Ask two students, "Do you like Mia Pearlman's paper art? Do you like the quilts from Gee's Bend? Do you like Gary LeMaster's eggshell sculptures?" After they answer, ask, "Why do you feel that way?" Then switch roles.

CREATE

Work in small groups. Ask and answer the questions. Use the vocabulary in **bold** and some of the words and phrases in parentheses.

1. Do you **like to draw**? If yes, what kinds of things do you **like to draw**?

2. Did you ever make any kind of art? What kind of art was it? (painting, **sculpture**, etc.) What **materials** did you use? Were they **unusual**?

3. In general, do **you like** art? What kind of art do **you like**? Why do **you like it**? (**I love, I like** _____/_____ **very much, I like** . . . , etc.)

4. Is there a kind of art that you **don't like**? If yes, what kind of art is it? Why don't you like it? (**I don't like, I can take it or leave it, I hate . . . ,** etc.)

5. Who is (or was) a great artist in your country? Do you **like** his/her art? Why or why not?

6. Do you have a **favorite** artist? If yes, is this artist's art **unusual**? What **materials** does this artist use? Does this artist have one **specific** work of art that is your **favorite**?

■■■■■■■■■■■■■■■■■■■■■■■■■■■■*GO TO* MyEnglishLab *FOR MORE VOCABULARY PRACTICE.*

GRAMMAR

1 Read the excerpts from the interview. Notice the verbs in **bold**.

a. WRITER: I'm very interested in Mia Pearlman's art.

b. GUIDE: When little girls **play** with dolls, like Barbie dolls, they usually **make up** stories about them.

c. GUIDE: **Do** you **see** that window?

d. GUIDE: And the sunlight from outside *really* **comes** through the window. . . . It **gives** the sculpture light.

    WRITER: So, the sculpture is like a part of nature inside the museum.

    GUIDE: Yes, and when you **stand** near the sculpture, you **feel** like you're a part of it, too.

e. GUIDE: I **know.** But Mia **thinks** sculptures are just like dances, or theater, or music concerts. You **enjoy** them, but they **don't last** forever. And that's life too—everything has an end.

f. WRITER: I have some specific questions about how Mia **makes** these sculptures.

(continued on next page)

Making Unusual Art   **45**

Look at the sentences on page 45.

1. Underline all the forms of the verbs **be** and **have**.

2. Look at all the other verbs.

    a. Which verbs end with **s**?

    b. Why?

    c. After the subjects *I, You,* and *They,* the verb (*ends with **s** / doesn't end with **s***).

THE SIMPLE PRESENT

1. Use the simple present tense for everyday actions or facts.	Mia Pearlman **makes** sculptures. The Gee's Bend women **make** quilts.
2. When the subject is the third-person singular— **he, she,** or **it**: put an *s* at the end of the main verb.	Paper **moves** and **changes**. (= It)
NOTE: After the subjects: **everything, something, nothing, anything** **everybody, somebody, nobody, anybody** use the third-person singular (*s* form).	*Everything* in the world **changes**.
NOTE: The verbs *be* and *have* are irregular.	**be:** *am, is, are* (See Unit 1.) **have:** I **have** some questions. The writer **has** some questions.
3. To form negative statements with contractions, use: *doesn't* or *don't* + the base form of the verb.	Paper **doesn't last** forever. The women in Gee's Bend **don't have** a plan for their quilts.
4. For *yes/no* questions, use: *Do* (or *Does*) + subject + the base form of the verb.	**Do** you **see** the window?
5. For *wh-* questions, use: *Wh-* word + *do* (or *does*) + subject + the base form of the verb.	**Why does** Mia Pearlman **use** paper?

2 Read the conversation silently. Fill in the correct form of the verb in parentheses in the simple present tense. Some verbs are negatives or questions. Remember, if the subject is third-person singular, you must add **s**.

Mia Pearlman and *Inrush*

MUSEUM GUIDE: Hello, everyone. This _____ Mia Pearlman's new
                                          1. (be)

sculpture. Its name _____ *Inrush*.
                          2. (be)

VISITOR 1: Excuse me. What _____ *Inrush* mean?
                                 3. (do)

GUIDE: Well, _____ you see the window up there? The
                  4. (do)

sunlight from outside always _____ into the
                                      5. (rush)

room and _____ the sculpture a lot of light. So
              6. (give)

the paper _____ like it is shining. This sculpture
                7. (look)

_____ that nature _____ a part of art.
      8. (show)   9. (be)

VISITOR 2: It _____ very beautiful, and it _____ so big!
                  10. (be)   11. (be)

How much time _____ Mia spend on each sculpture?
                      12. (do)

GUIDE: Well, it _____ on how big the sculpture is. Sometimes she
                      13. (depend)

_____ on one sculpture for a few months.
      14. (work)

(continued on next page)

VISITOR 1: And how long _____ her sculptures stay in the museum?
15. (do)

GUIDE: They usually _____ for a few weeks or months.
16. (stay)

VISITOR 1: And _____ they go to another museum after that?
17. (do)

GUIDE: No, Mia's sculptures _____ anywhere. When the show at
18. (neg. / go)

the museum _____, Mia _____ down all
19. (end)   20. (take)

the pieces of paper, and she _____ that sculpture together
21. (neg. / put)

again.

VISITOR 2: I _____ it!
22. (neg. / believe)

GUIDE: I _____! Many people _____ the same thing
23. (know)   24. (say)

when they _____ this.
25. (hear)

VISITOR 2: But I _____! Her sculptures _____
26. (neg. / understand)   27. (be)

beautiful! Why _____ she do that?
28. (do)

GUIDE: Mia _____ an unusual idea about sculpture. She
29. (have)

_____ her paper sculptures _____
30. (think)   31. (be)

like dances or theater or music performances. Those things

_____ forever. People _____ them and
32. (neg. / last)   33. (see)

_____ them, but then they _____ an end.
34. (enjoy)   35. (have)

That _____ life. Everything _____ an end.
36. (be)   37. (have)

Mia _____ that her art _____ the same. It
38. (believe)   39. (be)

_____ to last forever.
40. (neg. / have)

3 Read the conversation aloud with two classmates.

GO TO MyEnglishLab FOR MORE GRAMMAR PRACTICE.

PRONUNCIATION

FINAL INTONATION

At the end of a sentence, we use special *intonation*. This means that our voice may go up to a higher pitch or note ("rising" intonation), or it may go up and then down ("rising-falling" intonation).

When you:

a. make a **statement**

OR

b. ask a *wh-* question ("information question")

your voice **rises** (*goes up*) on the last stressed syllable, and then it **goes down** to a low sound.

Wh- question words include:

who, what, where, when, why, how, how much/many

To ask a *yes/no* question, your voice rises (*goes up*) on the last stressed word or after the last stressed syllable.

STATEMENTS:

(one-syllable word)

I only wanted to make the *place* where

Barbie **LIved**.

(two-syllable word)

Mia is an unusual **PERson**.

Wh- QUESTIONS:

(one-syllable word)

What do you **MEan**?

(two-syllable word)

What's going to happen to this **SCULPture**?

Yes / No QUESTIONS:

(one-syllable word)

Is that why her sculptures are so **BIG**?

(two-syllable word)

Do you see that **WINdow**?

---

1 🎧 Listen to the intonation at the end of these sentences. Does the speaker's voice go "up" or "up-down" on the last stressed word (marked in **bold**)? Circle the correct answer.

a. Mia's sculptures look like things we see in **nature**. (*up / up-down*)

b. What's going to **happen**? (*up / up-down*)

c. Is it going to a different **museum**? (*up / up-down*)

2 Look at the questions on page 49. Circle the correct answer or answers.

   a. Use rising-falling (up-down) intonation in (*statements* /***wh-*** *questions* / ***yes/no*** *questions*).

   b. Use rising (up) intonation in (*statements* /***wh-*** *questions* / ***yes/no*** *questions*).

3 Read the interview silently. Draw an arrow on the line at the end of each sentence. Show if the intonation goes up ➔ or up-down ⌒➘ on the last stressed word (marked in **bold**). The first few have been done for you.

WRITER: How does Mia Pearlman make her **sculptures**? ⌒ 1.

GUIDE: Well, first she goes to the museum or **gallery**. ⌒ 2.

   She looks at the space where the sculpture is going to **be**. ⌒ 3.

WRITER: Why does she **do** that? ⌒ 4.

GUIDE: She needs to know a few things, like, "How big is the **space**?" ⌒ 5.

   "Are there any **windows**?" 6.

   "Is there any **sunlight**?" 7.

WRITER: Why are those things **important**? 8.

GUIDE: Well, because the space is part of the **sculpture**. 9.

   Mia makes each one of her sculptures for only one specific **space**. 10.

WRITER: That's very **unusual**. 11.

   What does she do **next**? 12.

GUIDE: Next she goes back home, and she starts to **draw**. 13.

WRITER: What materials does she **use** for that? 14.

GUIDE: She just uses long pieces of white paper and black **ink**. 15.

   She draws all kinds of black lines on the **paper**. 16.

WRITER: Before she starts, does she have a specific **plan**? 17.

   Does she know what she wants to **draw**? 18.

GUIDE: No, she just draws what she feels at that **time**. 19.

4 Compare your arrows with your partner's and the teacher's. Then practice reading the conversation aloud with your partner. Pay special attention to use correct intonation.

SPEAKING SKILL

EXPRESSING OPINIONS

When we say our opinion, we often begin with a phrase such as "I think." Here are some other useful phrases:

In my opinion, . . .	I believe (that) . . .
If you ask me, . . .	I feel (that) . . .

I feel (that) Mia Pearlman's art is beautiful.

In my opinion, the Gee's Bend women are true artists.

If you ask me, eggshell sculpture is not real art.

I believe (that) art is a good way to express your ideas about the world.

Work with a partner. Student A: Tell Student B your opinion about the type of art in number 1. Begin with one of the phrases from the box. You can also add a sentence to say if you like it or not. Then ask Student B, "What do **you** think?" Student B: Explain your opinion. Begin with one of the phrases from the box. Then switch roles.

Example *Mia Pearlman's art*

STUDENT A: **In my opinion,** *Mia Pearlman's paper art is beautiful. I love it.*
                              (opinion)   (like/dislike)

                 What do **you** think?

STUDENT B: **I feel that** *it's very unusual. I like it a lot.*
                         (opinion)   (like/dislike)

1. modern art

    A: **If you ask me,** _____

       What do you think?

    B: _____

(continued on next page)

2. the eggshell sculpture

A: In my opinion, _____

What do you think?

B: _____

3. the Gee's Bend quilts

A: I feel _____

What do you think?

B: _____

4. Mia Pearlman's sculpture *Inrush*

A: I believe _____

What do you think?

B: _____

■■■■■■■■■■■■■■■*GO TO* MyEnglishLab *FOR MORE SKILL PRACTICE AND TO CHECK WHAT YOU LEARNED.*

FINAL SPEAKING TASK

A role play is a short performance. The students take on roles, or become characters, and act out a situation.

You are going to role-play a discussion about what kind of art to buy for a museum. Use the vocabulary, grammar, intonation, and phrases for expressing opinions from this unit.*

Role-play: Choosing Unusual Art for a Modern Art Museum.

You work for a Modern Art Museum. The Museum wants to buy one new piece of art. You are going to choose the art.

STEP 1: Meet in three groups:

Group 1: Mia Pearlman's paper sculpture

Group 2: a Gee's Bend quilt

Group 3: an eggshell sculpture

_____

* For Alternative Speaking Topics, see page 55.

In each group, look carefully at the picture(s) of your art and discuss these questions:

a. Is this art beautiful or interesting?

b. Is it difficult to make this art?

c. Does this art have a special meaning? What is it?

d. Did the artist use unusual material?

e. How will people feel when they see this art?

f. Why is this art important or special?

g. Why is this a good piece of art for a modern art museum?

STEP 2: Now, form new groups of three. Each new group has one person from each "art" group.

You and your partners work for the same modern art museum. You need to decide which type of art to buy for your museum. You can buy only one piece of art. Take turns speaking about the art you discussed in Step 1. Tell your partners why that art is the best one to buy. If anyone says, "That is not art," explain why it *is* art.

Listeners: Ask questions about the art your partners are describing.

STEP 3: Decide together which type of art you are going to buy for your museum.

STEP 4: Compare your answers with the other groups.

Group 1: Mia Pearlman's paper sculpture

"Eddy,"* a paper sculpture by Mia Pearlman

---

* an "eddy" is air or water that moves in a circle

Group 2: Gee's Bend quilt

A quilt made by Annie Mae Young from Gee's Bend, Alabama. Young used pieces of men's work clothes to make this quilt.

Group 3: Eggshell sculpture

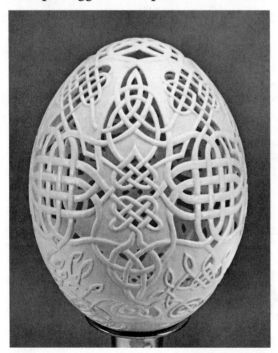

"1000 Celtic Dreams," an eggshell sculpture by Gary LeMaster

LeMaster used one continuous line to make the traditional Celtic design on this egg. It took him over 1000 hours to finish this sculpture. That's why he called it "1000 Celtic Dreams."

UNIT PROJECT

STEP 1: Work with a partner. Do research online about *traditional paper art* from one of these countries (or any other country that you are interested in):

China, Germany, India, Indonesia, Japan, Korea, Mexico, Poland, Turkey

STEP 2: Print some pictures or be prepared to show some online images of the type of art you researched.

STEP 3: Together with your partner, prepare to speak to your class for 3 minutes about what you learned. Don't memorize a speech. Just practice speaking about the type of paper art you researched.

Practice pronouncing the key words in your presentation before you speak. Ask your teacher to help you with this *before* your presentation.

STEP 4: Take turns speaking and presenting your pictures/photos to your classmates. Be sure to make eye contact with all of your classmates as you speak. Answer any questions that your classmates ask you.

Listening Task

Listen to your classmates' presentations. Ask them a question about something you don't understand completely, or ask them to give you more information

ALTERNATIVE SPEAKING TOPICS

1. Does your country have a traditional type of art (paper or other type)? What materials do people use to make it?

2. In your country, do students take art classes in school?

   a. If yes: At what age? (elementary school, junior high school, high school) Do the students *make* art, *learn about* art, or *study* famous art?

   b. If no: Is this OK? Why or why not?

   c. Is it important to have art classes in school? Why or why not?

3. Do you have any art in your room, apartment, or house? What kind of art is it? (paintings, posters, sculptures) What kind of art do you like to have in your home?

■ ■ ■ ■ ■ ■ ■ ■ ■ ■ ■ ■ ■ ■*GO TO* MyEnglishLab *TO DISCUSS ONE OF THE ALTERNATIVE TOPICS, WATCH A VIDEO ABOUT ART, AND TAKE THE UNIT 2 ACHIEVEMENT TEST.* ■

SPECIAL
Possessions

1 FOCUS ON THE TOPIC

1. Look at the photograph of dream catchers. What do people do with them? What culture do they come from?

2. A dream catcher is a special possession[1] to some people. What are some other special possessions?

3. Everyone dreams at night. Do you remember your dreams? Do you think dreams are important? Tell a partner about one of your dreams.

---

[1] **special possession:** something you keep because it is important to you

GO TO MyEnglishLab *TO CHECK WHAT YOU KNOW.*

VOCABULARY

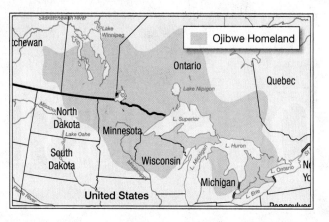

Ojibwe Homeland

Read and listen to the Web page about the Mille Lacs people of the Ojibwe Nation. Then match each boldfaced word to its definition on the next page.

Welcome to the culture page of
THE MILLE LACS PEOPLE

HOME

CONTACT

ABOUT US

We are a group of Ojibwe people living in the Mille Lacs area of Minnesota. Many years ago, the Ojibwe people lived in the Great Lakes area. Our **traditional** way of life was **peaceful** as we hunted, fished, and farmed. Then more people moved to our land from Europe and the United States. They came to our land with **modern** ways, and our life changed. These changes lasted for many years—they were not **temporary**. Some Ojibwe people became sick from European diseases and died. Also, our traditional **style** of government changed, and the young Ojibwe could not go to our schools anymore. They went to English-speaking schools. The Ojibwe people lost many important things. We lost our language and traditional stories. Some of us lost our life and **breath**! But today, things are different. We **protect** our culture in many ways. We send our older people into schools to teach children about Ojibwe life. At our Culture Center, we have **popular** classes on our language, history, and music. In the summer, we have our *powwow* tradition. This is a time for people to dance and sing together. We believe that dancing and singing are good for the **mind** and body. Body, mind, and music—a powwow brings everything together.

Please visit our Culture Center to learn more about the Mille Lacs people. We **appreciate** your interest.

_____ 1. breath   **a.** liked by many people

_____ 2. mind   **b.** new

_____ 3. modern   **c.** pattern or design

_____ 4. peaceful   **d.** to keep safe

_____ 5. popular   **e.** air coming into or out of the mouth or nose

_____ 6. protect   **f.** coming from the past

_____ 7. style   **g.** understand that something is good and important

_____ 8. temporary   **h.** the thinking part of humans

_____ 9. traditional   **i.** not fighting or worrying

_____ 10. appreciate   **j.** not lasting

GO TO MyEnglishLab *FOR MORE VOCABULARY PRACTICE.*

PREVIEW

1 How do you think people make dream catchers? Discuss this question with a partner.

web →

← feather

2 🎧 Listen to the excerpt from "The Story of Dream Catchers." Read the sentences. Check (✓) **Yes**, **No**, or **I Don't Know**. Discuss your answers with a partner.

	Yes	No	I Don't Know
1. A dream catcher has a web.	☑	☐	☐
2. The web has holes at the top.	☐	☐	☐
3. The meaning of the web is "life."	☐	☐	☐

MAIN IDEAS

1 🎧 Listen to the whole story. Look at your answers from the Preview on page 59. Did they help you to understand the story?

2 Read the sentences. Put the sentences in order from 1 to 7. Follow the order that you hear in the story. The first one has been done for you.

_____ **a.** The traditional dream catcher comes from the story of Spider Woman.

_____ **b.** People buy dream catchers for their friends.

_____ **c.** The Ojibwe people move to other parts of North America.

__1__ **d.** The Ojibwe people tell traditional stories about Spider Woman.

_____ **e.** The traditional place to put a dream catcher is over your bed.

_____ **f.** Mothers and grandmothers make dream catchers for babies.

_____ **g.** A dream catcher stops bad dreams and lets good dreams enter the mind.

DETELS

1. The story of dream catchers is a/an _____.

   a. Ojibwe story

   b. modern story

2. Webs are part of dream catchers because of _____.

   a. North America

   b. Spider Woman

3. Dream catchers protect babies. They let in _____.

   a. good dreams

   b. bad dreams

4. Many modern dream catchers are _____ traditional ones.

   a. different from

   b. the same as

5. Powerful dreams are good for _____.

   a. our dream catchers

   b. our minds

6. Big dream catchers in stores are not _____.

   a. popular

   b. traditional

■■■■■■■■■■■■■■■■■■■■■■■■■■■■ GO TO MyEnglishLab FOR MORE LISTENING PRACTICE.

MAKE INFERENCES

UNDERSTANDING A SPEAKER'S BELIEFS

An inference is a guess about something that is not directly stated. To make an inference, use information that you understand from what you hear.

We can make inferences about a speaker's beliefs. To do this, we listen for important words. These words help us to understand the speaker's beliefs.

🎧 Listen to the example. What does the speaker believe about dreams?

Example

SPEAKER'S BELIEF: Both good and bad dreams are _____.

a. powerful

b. good for sleeping

The correct answer is: **a.** The word *protect* helps us to understand the speaker's belief that both good and bad dreams have power. Bad dreams have the power to hurt us, and good dreams have the power to keep us safe.

🎧 Listen to each excerpt from the lecture. Pay attention to the speaker's words and think about the speaker's beliefs. Circle the correct word or phrase to complete the sentence.

Excerpt One

1. The speaker believes:

Dreams have the power to change our way of _____.

a. thinking

b. feeling

Excerpt Two

2. The speaker believes:

It is beau 🖑 l to remember our friends' _____.

a. love

b. gifts

3. The speaker believes:

It is not helpful to use a dream catcher _____.

a. for driving

b. for sleeping

EXPRESS OPINIONS

Do you agree or disagree with the statements? Circle your answer. Then discuss your answers in a small group. Explain your opinions.

1. Dream catchers can help everyone, not only Native Americans. Agree **Disagree**

2. It's important to protect people from bad dreams. Agree **Disagree**

3. It's OK to change our traditional ways. Agree **Disagree**

GO TO MyEnglishLab TO GIVE YOUR OPINION ABOUT ANOTHER QUESTION.

Special Possessions 63

COMPREHENSION

Two college students are moving into a room in the dormitory, which is a large building with rooms for students. Another student joins them. They have a conversation about their special possessions.

🎧 **Listen to the conversation and read the statements. Mark each statement T (true) or F (false). Correct the false statements.**

_____ **1.** At the beginning, both Sara and Amber are happy about the toy bear.

_____ **2.** Lucy the bear goes everywhere with Lauren.

_____ **3.** Lucy is a new toy bear.

_____ **4.** Amber doesn't keep old things.

_____ **5.** Sara has a lucky dream catcher to help her pass tests.

VOCABULARY

1 Read the conversation and notice the words in bold.

STUDENT 1: Why are you wearing a red baseball cap?

STUDENT 2: It's my **good luck charm**. It helps me pass tests.

STUDENT 1: That's **cool**. I have a lucky ring. See? It was my grandmother's ring. She had it for a long time and then she **passed** it **down** to me. I wear it all the time because I love her so much. It has a lot of **sentimental value** to me.

STUDENT 2: Nice. I think my sister has our grandmother's old ring. She keeps everything! Old books, old toys, everything. She's a **pack rat**.

STUDENT 1: My brother is a pack rat, too. He keeps all his old clothes, but he never wears them!

STUDENT 2: My sister's like that too . . .

2 Complete the sentences by matching each sentence beginning on the left with the correct ending on the right. Write the letter of the correct ending on the line.

_____ 1. If you are a pack rat . . .	**a.** nice or good.
_____ 2. Things with sentimental value . . .	**b.** you always save your old things.
_____ 3. If someone passes a ring down . . .	**c.** good luck.
_____ 4. A good luck charm brings us . . .	**d.** help us remember family and friends.
_____ 5. Something "cool" is . . .	**e.** it goes from older to younger family members.

■■■■■■■■■■■■■■■■■■■■■■■■■■■■■ *GO TO* MyEnglishLab *FOR VOCABULARY PRACTICE.*

UNDERSTANDING A SPEAKER'S EXCITEMENT

When speakers are very excited about a topic, they often speak louder. They sometimes pronounce words more slowly or with a higher voice. When speakers are not excited about a topic, their voices do not change very much. They pronounce all the words in the same way.

Understanding a speaker's excitement is part of understanding how he or she feels about the topic. When we understand a speaker's feeling, we can have a better conversation because we understand the other person's opinion and point of view.

🎧 Listen to the example. Is the speaker excited? How do you know?

Example

LAUREN: Lucy has a lot of sentimental value. She was my grandmother's bear for *a long time*. Then my grandmother gave her to my mom, and my mom passed her down to *me*!

1. Is the speaker excited?

_____ **a.** Yes

_____ **b.** No

2. How do you know? Which words are louder, higher, or spoken more slowly?

The correct answers are: 1. **a**, 2. The speaker says *a long time* louder and more slowly. She says *to me* in a higher and louder voice.

Explanation

When Lauren uses a louder voice and pronounces words more slowly, she emphasizes the importance of Lucy, the toy bear. She is excited that her grandmother and mother gave her something so important and with such sentimental value.

Listen to the excerpts from Toys in College. Is the speaker excited? Listen to the speaker's voice. Is it loud? Is it high? Does the speaker pronounce some words more slowly than others?

Excerpt One

1. Is the speaker excited?

_____ a. Yes

_____ b. No

2. How do you know? Which words are louder, higher, or spoken more slowly?

_____

Excerpt Two

1. Is the speaker excited?

_____ a. Yes

_____ b. No

2. How do you know? Which words are louder, higher, or spoken more slowly?

_____

Excerpt Three

1. Is the speaker excited?

_____ a. Yes

_____ b. No

2. How do you know? Which words are louder, higher, or spoken more slowly?

_____

■■■■■■■■■■■■■■■■■■■■■■■■■■■■■■■■■ GO TO MyEnglishLab FOR MORE SKILL PRACTICE.

STEP 1: Organize

Why are special possessions important? Look at the list of reasons. Complete the chart by writing three reasons under "Dream Catchers" (Listening One) and three reasons under "Toys in College" (Listening Two).

List of Reasons

- part of families for many years
- lucky
- traditional
- helps you feel happy and peaceful
- sentimental value
- many styles

DREAM CATCHERS	TOYS IN COLLEGE
1.	1.
2.	2.
3.	3.

STEP 2: Synthesize

Work with a partner. Student A, you are a news reporter. You will interview Student B about a new game called Special Possessions. Student B, you are the designer of the game. Explain to Student A why special possessions are important to people. Use reasons from the chart in Step 1: Organize to answer. Then explain your answers by speaking about an example.

Example

Special possessions are important because they have many styles. Dream catchers are a good example because some are very big. Some have beautiful feathers.

REPORTER: Why did you make this game? Do you really think that people will like to play a game about special possessions?

DESIGNER: Yes. Special possessions are important to people because . . .

(*Give one reason from the chart.*) _____.
1.

REPORTER: Really? Can you give me an example of that?

DESIGNER: Well, I think a good example is _____ because . . .
2.

(*Speak about an example.*)

REPORTER: What about good luck charms? Are they special possessions, too?

DESIGNER: For some people, yes. Sometimes people use things in a new way because they want to be lucky. For example, some people _____.
3.
(*Speak about an example.*)

Now switch roles. Student B, you are the news reporter. You will ask Student A questions. Student A, you are the game designer. Use information from the chart in Step 1: Organize to answer. If you repeat information, you can begin with, "As I explained before . . ."

REPORTER: So, special possessions are sometimes important to people because they bring good luck. What about things that people pass down in their families?

DESIGNER:

Those things are important, too. Those are things with _____. They are important because . . .
4.

(*Choose the correct reason.*)

REPORTER: Can you give me an example?

DESIGNER: Well, one example is _____. This is important because . . .
5.
(*Speak about an example.*)

Also, people sometimes like things with many different styles. For example

_____.
6.
(*Speak about an example.*)

REPORTER: Yes—that's true. What about people who keep old things—you know books, toys, old newspapers . . .

DESIGNER: I have another idea for those people. I want to make a game called Pack Rat!

■■■■■■■■■■■■■■■■■■■■■■■■■■■■■■■GO TO MyEnglishLab *TO CHECK WHAT YOU LEARNED.*

VOCABULARY

REVIEW

A professional organizer helps people make their homes more organized. In an organized home, it is easy to find things. Everything has a place, and there are no extra things. Read the Web page of a professional organizer and fill in the blanks with the words from the box. You will not use all of the words.

appreciate	good luck charms	pack rat	sentimental value
breath	mind	peaceful	style
cool	modern	popular	traditional

GET ORGANIZED!

HOME

CONTACT

ABOUT US

Are you a _____ with too many things? Do you want to feel
1.

more _____ in your home? Do you want to think with a clear
2.

_____? I can help. I am a professional organizer for this busy
3.

_____ world. I can make your house a very _____
    4.   5.

place for you and your friends. They will love it! (And it's sometimes true—a

nice, organized house will make you more _____ with friends.)
                                           6.

Listen—I know that organizing is hard. I understand that some of your things have

_____, and you want to keep them. That's fine with me. You can
    7.

keep your special possessions and _____. I will not tell you what to
                                      8.

do. That's not my _____. But I *will* organize your home—and you
                     9.

will _____ the changes. Just click below to contact me today.
       10.

EXPAND

1 Work with a partner. Read the conversation between a professional organizer and a
pack rat. Notice the words in bold.

PROFESSIONAL ORGANIZER: OK, let's get started. What is something that you don't need
anymore? What do you want to **get rid of**?

PACK RAT: I'm not sure. I don't like to throw things away. Maybe I will
need them later. Then what will I do?

PROFESSIONAL ORGANIZER: Don't worry about that. Let's think about today. What about
this old bike? Do you want to keep it?

PACK RAT: Yes. It's my first bike. It's very important to me.

PROFESSIONAL ORGANIZER: OK. You want to **hold on to** it. That's fine. What about
these old math books? Do you still need them?

PACK RAT: Not today . . . but maybe in the future—

PROFESSIONAL ORGANIZER: I really don't think you will need them in the future. Why
don't we **give** them **away**?

PACK RAT: To who?

PROFESSIONAL ORGANIZER: I'm sure we can find someone—maybe a teacher or old
book **collector**. Or maybe somebody wants to **recycle**
them. Let's keep going . . .

2 Match the words and phrases to their definitions.

_____ 1. recycle

_____ 2. collector

_____ 3. get rid of something

_____ 4. give something away

_____ 5. hold on to something

a. keep something

b. use something again

c. a person who gets and keeps similar things (books, stamps, jewelry)

d. not keep something

e. give something to another person

CREATE

Discuss these questions with a partner. Student A, ask questions 1–3. Student B, ask questions 4–6. Prepare to share interesting answers with the class.

1. Are you a collector? What do you collect?

2. Are you a pack rat? Is it hard for you to get rid of things? Explain.

3. How often do you give things away? What do you give away?

4. Do you want a professional organizer to help you at home? Why or why not?

5. Do you have any good luck charms? Do they help you?

6. What kinds of things have sentimental value in your life?

GO TO MyEnglishLab FOR MORE VOCABULARY PRACTICE.

GRAMMAR

1 Read the sentences. Then answer the questions.

a. The book collector often shops online.

b. Old traditional ways always change.

c. I never keep old things.

d. Do you usually put a dream catcher near your bed?

e. It is always expensive[2] to collect cars.

f. Professional organizers are sometimes very busy.

_____

[2] **expensive:** costing a lot of money

1. Which words are adverbs of frequency? Underline them.

2. Where do adverbs go with the verb **be**?

3. Where do adverbs go with all other verbs?

THE SIMPLE PRESENT WITH ADVERBS OF FREQUENCY

1. Use adverbs of frequency to show how often something happens or how often people do things.	Always: 100% of the time Usually: 90% of the time Often: 70% of the time Sometimes: 30% of the time Never: 0% of the time
2. When the verb is *be*, put the adverb of frequency after the verb.	The students are **never** late to class. A toy bear is **always** cute. The style of a dream catcher is **sometimes** modern.
3. With all other verbs, put the adverb of frequency before the verb.	He **often** keeps his old books. She **usually** looks for rings online.
4. For *yes/no* and *wh-* questions, put the adverb before the verb. You can also ask about frequency by using *How often . . . ?*	Does she **often** buy toys? Is a dream catcher **always** expensive? What do they **usually** collect? **How often** do you remember your dreams?
5. In negative statements, put *don't* and *doesn't* before the adverb of frequency. Use *ever* instead of *never*. In negative statements with the verb *be*, put the adverb of frequency after the verb *be*.	They don't **often** go shopping. He doesn't **always** keep old things. She doesn't **ever** take off her ring. We aren't **usually** late to class. Clothing isn't **always** expensive.

2 Sara and Amber are listening to a college lecture on special possessions. Complete the sentences with the correct adverb of frequency.

PROFESSOR: We know that people _____ have special possessions, but

                                   1. (often /never)

why? The reasons depend on the person. For example, an 80-year-old

grandmother loves her old ring. She _____ shows it to her

                                   2. (never /sometimes)

grandson, but he doesn't think the ring is important. He is more interested

(continued on next page)

in his guitar or basketball. We understand this difference clearly. But, it is an interesting question: Why do people _____ like different kinds
3. (never /usually)
of things? Can anyone tell me why?

AMBER: Is it because of different ages? I mean, the grandmother is old, and the grandson is young, so they _____ like the same things.
4. (never /always)

PROFESSOR: Well, that's possible, but according to one study, it's because of **male and female**[3] differences. Males and females _____ keep things
5. (often /never)
for different reasons. Let's think about a boy in high school: he holds on to a basketball and an old guitar—why? Both of these things are useful. They help him do things. They make him feel important. But girls in high school _____ get more excited about a toy bear or a ring from a
6. (always /usually)
friend.

SARA: Why is that? Doesn't she want to feel important, too?

PROFESSOR: I'm sure she does, but the ring and the bear _____ have
7. (usually /never)
sentimental value. Things with sentimental value _____ help
8. (sometimes /always)
us remember important people in our lives. This is very important to the high school girl. That's why she doesn't _____ want to throw
9. (never /ever)
these things away! Both males and females enjoy their special possessions, but their reasons are _____ different.
10. (often /sometimes)

---

[3] **male and female:** boy and girl, man and woman

3 Work with a partner. Take turns describing a special possession—something you have and keep because it is very important to you. Answer these questions:

- What does it look like?
- Where does it come from?
- Is it useful? Is it beautiful?

- Where do you usually keep it?
- How do you usually take care of it?
- How often do you look at it or use it?
- How often do you show it to others?

■■■■■■■■■■■■■■■■■■■■■■■■■■■■■■■■GO TO MyEnglishLab FOR MORE GRAMMAR PRACTICE.

PRONUNCIATION

1 🎧 Listen to the underlined verbs in the conversation. The present tense ending **-s** has three different pronunciations.

A: Your mother has a beautiful ring!

B: She <u>loves</u> that ring. She only <u>takes</u> it off to clean it.

A: Clean it? How do you clean a ring?

B: With toothpaste! She <u>brushes</u> her ring with toothpaste.

Look at the three underlined verbs in the conversation. Answer this question for each verb: Does the -s ending add a new syllable or just a new sound?

PRONOUNCING -*S* ENDINGS FOR PRESENT TENSE	
In the present tense, the pronunciation of the third-person singular ending depends on the last sound of the *base form* of the verb.	
1. Pronounce the -*s* ending /əz/ or /ɪz/ after /s/, /z/, **sh** and **ch** and **j**. (See the phonetic alphabet on page 236.) After these sounds, the -*s* ending adds a new syllable.	use (one syllable) → uses (two syllables) She **uses** toothpaste to clean her ring. Tom **washes** his new car every day. The professor **teaches** the students on Mondays.
2. Pronounce the -*s* ending /s/ after /p, t, k, f /. The -*s* ending is a final sound.	She **keeps** her rings in a special box. He **wants** to keep his old guitar. The ring **looks** beautiful.
3. Pronounce the -*s* ending /z/ after **all other sounds**. The -*s* ending is a final sound.	She never **wears** rings. The student **stays** at school all day. The professor **arrives** at 8:00 A.M.

2 🎧 Listen to the conversation and repeat the lines. Then practice the conversation with a partner.

A: My roommate's a jewelry collector. Tonight she **wants** to watch a video about Native American jewelry. Do you want to see it with us?

B: Sure. What time? My class **ends** at 7:30, but the professor never **finishes** on time. Sometimes she **teaches** until 8:00 P.M.!

A: No problem. We're going to watch it online. Just come when she **lets** you out.

B: OK. Is the video long? I have an early class in the morning.

A: I don't think it's long. It probably **lasts** about an hour.

B: Good. I'll see you tonight.

3 Circle the pronunciation of the **-s** ending of the underlined words. Then check your answers with a classmate's and take turns reading the sentences. The first one has been done for you.

1. Lauren <u>wears</u> her ring all the time. It <u>looks</u> expensive.
      əz / s / (z)   əz / s / z

2. George <u>buys</u> and <u>sells</u> expensive jewelry. He <u>travels</u> all over the world.
     əz / s / z   əz / s / z   əz / s / z

3. My roommate really <u>likes</u> toy animals. She <u>gets</u> something new every week.
         əz / s / z   əz /(s)/ z

4. The movie *Dream Catchers* <u>starts</u> at 2:00. It <u>takes</u> about an hour to get there, so let's
               əz / s / z   əz /(s)/ z
   leave before 1:00.

5. The book store <u>opens</u> at 10 A.M. and <u>closes</u> at 6:00 P.M.
       əz / s / z   əz / s / z

STUDENT B	TIMES	
1. The hours of the video about Ojibwe people	2. P.M.	2. P.M.
2. The hours of the Ojibwe Museum store	11:00	5:00 P.M.
3. The hours of the bus to the dream catcher store (verbs: *leave, arrive*)	1:00 P.M.	2:00 P.M.
4. The hours of the story telling by George Wolf (verbs: *start, end*)	3:00 P.M.	4:00 P.M.

4 Work with a partner. Student A, you want to learn more about dream catchers. Student B, you want to learn more about the Ojibwe people. Student A, look at the information below. Student B, look at the information at the bottom of page 76. Use the model to ask your partner for the missing information. Then write the information in your chart. Student A, use the verbs in your chart to tell your partner the information that she / he is missing. Then switch roles. Student B will begin by asking questions. Look at the example:

Example

B: Do you know the hours of the Ojibwe Museum?

A: Yes, *it opens at 10:00 A.M. and closes at 6:00 P.M.*

/z/ /əz/

STUDENT A	TIMES	
The hours of the Ojibwe Museum	10:00 A.M.	6:00 P.M.

STUDENT B	TIMES	
The hours of the Ojibwe Museum	_____	_____

STUDENT A	TIMES	
1. The hours of the video about Ojibwe people (verbs: *begin, end*)	2:00 P.M.	3:00 P.M.
2. The hours of the Ojibwe Museum store (verbs: *open, close*)	11:00 A.M.	5:00 P.M.
3. The hours of the bus to the dream catcher store	1:00 PM	1:00 PM
4. The hours of the story telling by George Wolf	5:00 PM	9:00 PM

SPEAKING SKILL

ASKING QUESTIONS TO INCLUDE OTHERS IN A DISCUSSION

A good speaker knows how to include others by asking questions. These questions allow others to join a discussion. They give other people a chance to talk.

🎧 Listen to the example.

Example

LAUREN: Lucy isn't just a toy. She's a part of my life—and part of my family, too. What about you? Don't you have any special possessions?

The first question invites the other person to speak. The second question begins with *don't*. This means that the speaker expects the other person to say "yes." Questions that begin with a negative auxiliary (*don't/doesn't/isn't/aren't*) mean that the speaker expects the other person to agree or say "yes." Look at these examples:

A: **Don't** you think teddy bears are cute?

B: Yes, I do.

A: **Isn't** this pen lucky?

B: Yes, it is.

Other questions begin with affirmative auxiliaries (*do/does/is/are*). These questions mean that the speaker wants information. The speaker does not expect the other person to agree or say "yes." Look at these examples:

A: **Do** you have a teddy bear?

B: No, I don't.

A: **Is** this pen lucky?

B: I don't know.

1 🎧 Listen to the examples from Listening Two. Underline the questions in each one. Then listen again and repeat the questions.

1. Old things really aren't that important to me. How about you, Sara?

2. It stops the bad dreams. It only lets the good dreams come into your mind. Isn't it beautiful?

3. Is it a good luck charm? Does it help you to pass tests?

4. When I take notes with my lucky pen, I usually get As! What about you—do you ask the big bear for help with your tests?

a horseshoe

a rabbit's foot

a four-leaf clover

2 What do you know about good luck charms in North America? Look at the photos. Complete the discussion by writing questions in the blanks. Then read the conversation with a partner. Switch roles and repeat the conversation.

- Isn't that a plant with four leaves?
- Can you think of other good luck charms?
- How about you?
- Isn't that lucky?

STUDENT 1: I want to buy a rabbit's foot.

STUDENT 2: Why?

STUDENT 1: It's good luck.

STUDENT 2: Really? A rabbit's foot?

STUDENT 1: Not a real one—a synthetic[4] one.

STUDENT 2: Oh, I see. Well, I need some good luck, too. I have a lot of tests this week.
_____
1.

STUDENT 1: I have a lot of tests, too.

STUDENT 2: What other good luck charms do you know about?

STUDENT 1: Well, there's a little plant . . .

STUDENT 2: A clover? _____
2.

STUDENT 1: Yes. It brings good luck. What about you? _____
3.

STUDENT 2: How about a horseshoe? _____
4.

STUDENT 1: You're right—it is. Maybe we can buy one. We need to pass our tests!

_____
[4] **synthetic:** made by humans; not natural

■ ■ ■ ■ ■ ■ ■ ■ ■ ■ ■ *GO TO* MyEnglishLab *FOR MORE SKILL PRACTICE AND TO CHECK WHAT YOU LEARNED.*

FINAL SPEAKING TASK

In this task, you will have a discussion about the reasons for holding on to special possessions. Try to use the vocabulary, grammar, pronunciation, and signal words that you learned in this unit.*

Work in small groups of three or four. Follow the steps.

STEP 1: Imagine that there is a fire in your home. You need to leave very quickly. You only have time to take one special possession with you. First, make a list of several special possessions in your home. Then look at the list of questions. Use the questions to decide which special possession you will take. Tell your group your decision and explain your reasons.

- Is it useful?
- Is it beautiful?
- Is it a traditional part of the family?
- Is it a good luck charm?
- Does it have sentimental value?
- Is it expensive?

STEP 2: Choose one reporter for your group. The reporter will mark each reason to see how many times students in your group discuss it. Then the reporter will tell the class about each decision and which reasons were the most important in your group.

Example

- Is it useful? IIII
- Is it beautiful? III
- Is it a traditional part of the family? I
- Is it a good luck charm? I
- Does it have sentimental value? II
- Is it expensive? III

Listening Task

Listen to the reporters from each group. What are the reasons for each decision? Which reasons did students choose most often? Which reasons do you agree and disagree with? Discuss your opinions with a partner.

---

* For Alternative Speaking Topics, see page 81.

UNIT PROJECT

STEP 1: Interview a classmate about a special possession that belongs to his or her family. Ask these questions:

- Why is this possession special to your family?
- Where does it come from?
- Who keeps it?
- Who takes care of it?
- What will happen to this possession in the future? Who will you pass it down to?
- *Your own question*

STEP 2: Use the Internet to find pictures of this kind of possession and more information.

STEP 3: Tell the class about your classmate's special possession. Share the most interesting information about it.

ALTERNATIVE SPEAKING TOPICS

Discuss one of the topics with the class. Use the vocabulary and grammar from the unit.

1. Imagine that you have the chance to collect anything. What will you collect? Why?

2. Antique furniture can be hundreds of years old. Some people like it and spend a lot of money on it. What kind of furniture do you like—antique or modern? Explain.

3. Pack rats usually hold on to everything, not only their special possessions. What is your advice to pack rats? How can they learn to get rid of things or give them away?

4. What are some good luck charms in your home culture? Do you believe that they bring good luck to people? How often do you use them? Explain.

■ ■ ■ ■ ■ ■ ■ ■ ■ ■ ■ ■ *GO TO* MyEnglishLab *TO DISCUSS ONE OF THE ALTERNATIVE TOPICS, WATCH A VIDEO ABOUT A STOLEN WEDDING DRESS, AND TAKE THE UNIT 3 ACHIEVEMENT TEST.* ■ ■ ■ ■ ■ ■ ■ ■ ■ ■ ■ ■ ■

CREATIVITY IN
Business

1 FOCUS ON THE TOPIC

1. Look at the photo and the title. How old is the person in the photo? What is she doing? What does the title mean?

2. Creative people have new and different ideas. What kinds of businesses need creative workers?

3. Children are usually creative when they play. They have new ideas, and they create, or make, new things. When you were a child, what creative things did you do? Did you ever make or sell anything?

GO TO MyEnglishLab *TO CHECK WHAT YOU KNOW.*

LISTENING ONE KK GREGORY, YOUNG AND CREATIVE

VOCABULARY

1 🎧 Many big companies are teaching their employees to be more creative. Read and listen to this article from an online business magazine.

Can Employees Learn to Be More *Creative*? Many Business Owners Say "YES!"

Big companies, like American Express®, Microsoft®, FedEx Office®, and Disney®, want their **employees** to be **creative**—to think in new and interesting ways. These companies pay billions of dollars for **creativity** classes for their employees.

In some creativity classes, employees play games together in a classroom. In other classes, they do **exciting** sports together outside. For example, at the Playtime Company, a **successful** advertising company, employees go white-water rafting and rock climbing together. All of these activities help employees to think in new ways.

In creativity classes, teachers also give employees important **advice**:

- Relax. When people relax, they can think better.

- Don't be **afraid** to **make mistakes**. No one is perfect. Just try to do your best. Great ideas sometimes come from mistakes.

- Think young! Children are very creative, so sometimes we need to think like children.

When employees have creative ideas, companies become more successful. One successful business owner said, "One creativity class helped my employees more than many years of work **experience**." Many other big business **owners** agree. Creativity classes are helping their companies.

2 **A.** Circle all of the choices that correctly complete the sentence. Then check your answers with your teacher.

The article says that when employees relax and play games, they can

_____.

a. make a lot of money

b. get creative ideas for work

c. be more active

d. lose their jobs

e. think in new ways

f. feel afraid to make mistakes

B. Take turns with a partner. Student A, read the sentence and choose the correct meaning of the word from the magazine article. Student B, say, "Yes, I agree" or "No, I don't think so. I think . . ."

Example

Employees are (*people who work for a company / people who don't have jobs*).

A: Employees are *people who work for a company*.

B: Yes, I agree.

OR

A: **Employees** are *people who don't have jobs*.

B: No, I don't think so. I think employees are *people who work for a company*.

1. **A:** A **creative** person is a person who has (*new and interesting ideas / the same ideas as other people*).

   B: (Yes, I agree. / No, I don't think so. I think it is a person who has . . .)

2. **A:** Business **owners** are people who (*work for a business / have their own business*).

   B: (Yes, I agree. / No, I don't think so. I think they are people who . . .)

3. **A:** **Creativity** means having ideas that (*can make a lot of money / are new and different*).

   B: (Yes, I agree. / No, I don't think so. I think it means having ideas that . . .)

(continued on next page)

4. **A:** **Exciting** things (*are a lot of fun / cost a lot of money*).

   B: (Yes, I agree. / No, I don't think so. I think they are . . .)

5. **A:** A **successful** company is a company that (*makes a lot of money / has many employees*).

   B: (Yes, I agree. / No, I don't think so. I think it is a company that . . .)

6. **A:** When you give **advice**, you give (*information to help another person / information about yourself*).

   B: (Yes, I agree. / No, I don't think so. I think it means you give . . .)

7. **A:** To be **afraid** means to be nervous and scared because (*something is very boring / something is difficult or different*).

   B: (Yes, I agree. / No, I don't think so. I think it means to be nervous and scared because . . .)

8. **A:** When you **make mistakes**, you do something (*the right way / the wrong way*).

   B: (Yes, I agree. / No, I don't think so. I think it means you do something . . .)

9. **A:** When you have work **experience**, it means you (*worked at a job / got a new job*).

   B: (Yes, I agree. / No, I don't think so. I think it means you . . .)

■ GO TO MyEnglishLab *FOR MORE VOCABULARY PRACTICE.*

PREVIEW

🎧 Listen to the beginning of "KK Gregory, Young and Creative." Then circle your idea.

Professor Jason Chandler teaches an MBA (Master's in Business Administration) class at a California university. He invited KK Gregory to speak to his class. KK is a high school student. She has her own business. It is called Wristies.

Why does Professor Chandler want KK to speak to his business students?

a. The business students will enjoy listening to KK's talk.

b. The business students can learn from KK's experience.

c. The business students can get jobs at KK's company.

GRADUATE SCHOOL OF BUSINESS

SPECIAL LECTURE!
"Personal Creativity in Business"
Guest speaker: KK Gregory

9:00–11:00
Room 121
Prof. J. Chandler

BUS G341
Course

MAIN IDEAS

1 🎧 Listen to KK Gregory's talk. Look at your answer from Preview on page 87. Was it correct? Did it help you to understand KK's talk?

2 🎧 Listen again. Read the sentences. Write **T** (true) or **F** (false). Correct the false sentences.

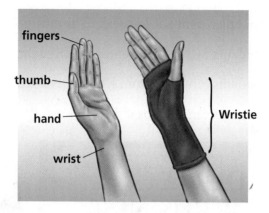

_____ 1. KK started her business when she was 17 years old.

_____ 2. Wristies keep your fingers warm.

_____ 3. KK's mother helped her to make the first pair of Wristies.

_____ 4. KK's mother didn't have any business experience.

_____ 5. KK thinks it's important to do new things.

DETAILS

🎧 Listen again. **Two** answers are correct. Cross out the **incorrect** answer. Read the correct sentences aloud. The first one has been done for you.

1. When you wear Wristies, _____.

    a. ~~your thumbs are covered~~

    b. your wrists are warm

    c. you can move your fingers

2. KK made the first pair of Wristies _____.

    a. because she didn't have gloves

    b. on a snowy day

    c. when she was 10 years old

3. KK's friends _____.

   a. really liked their Wristies

   b. wanted to sell their Wristies

   c. wore their Wristies every day

4. KK thought about starting a business _____.

   a. because her friends suggested it

   b. after her mother said it was a good idea

   c. when she made the first pair of Wristies

5. When KK started the Wristies company, _____.

   a. her mother helped her

   b. her mother had a store

   c. she had a few problems

6. People can buy Wristies _____.

   a. in many stores

   b. on the Internet

   c. at the supermarket

7. When KK went on a TV shopping show, _____.

   a. she was very successful

   b. she sold 6,000 pairs of Wristies

   c. she was nervous and excited

8. KK's advice to the business students is to _____.

   a. be creative

   b. do new things

   c. start your own business

■■■■■■■■■■■■■■■■■■■■■■■■■■■■■■■GO TO MyEnglishLab FOR MORE LISTENING PRACTICE.

MAKE INFERENCES

NOTICING CONTRASTING IDEAS

An inference is a guess about something that is not directly stated. To make an inference, use information that you understand from what you hear.

In English, when we stress a word, we say it *louder, longer*, and with *higher pitch*. When we want to show that there is an important difference, or contrast, between two things or ideas, we give the two contrasting (different) words the strongest stress in the sentence. These words are stressed *more* than the *other stressed* words. Noticing the stressed words helps us understand the speaker's meaning.

🎧 Listen to the sentence. All the stressed words are in CAPITAL letters. The words with contrastive stress are in **BOLD CAPITALS**.

Example

KK: It's REALLY EXCITING to be here, in a **BUSINESS** SCHOOL CLASS, because I'M STILL in **HIGH** SCHOOL!

Which two words is KK contrasting? _____ and _____

Why? KK wants to explain that:

a. Business school is very exciting.

b. It's very unusual for a high school student to speak to business school students.

Answers: KK is contrasting the words **BUSINESS** and **HIGH**.
Why? The correct answer is **b.** It's very unusual for a high school student to speak to business school students.

Explanation   By using contrastive stress on the words **BUSINESS** and **HIGH**, KK is explaining that these two kinds of schools are very different. Notice that we do not place extra stress on the word that is the same: SCHOOL.

🎧   Listen to each excerpt from the talk. Write down the two words that KK is contrasting in each sentence. Then choose the sentence that explains the idea she is trying to express.

Excerpt One

1. Which two words is KK contrasting? _____ and _____

2. What does KK want to explain?

   a. She is young now, but when she started her company, she was much younger.

   b. KK has worked at her company for a very long time.

1. Which two words is KK contrasting? _____ and _____

2. What does KK want to explain?

   a. The gloves are very long.

   b. Most gloves have fingers, but Wristies do not have fingers.

1. Which two words is KK contrasting? _____ and _____

2. What does KK want to explain?

   a. Most people only wear gloves outside, but people can wear Wristies inside, too.

   b. Wristies are good for sports but also for work.

1. Which two words is KK contrasting? _____ and _____

2. What does KK want to explain?

   a. Her warm clothes and gloves did not cover her wrists.

   b. KK's wrists were always cold in the winter.

EXPRESS OPINIONS

Work with a partner. Answer the questions.

1. KK told the business students, "Don't be afraid to try something new." Did you ever feel afraid to do something new? Tell about your experience. Did you do it? If yes, how did you feel? If no, was it the right decision?

2. "KK's mother made an excellent decision. It's very good for a child to have a business." Do you agree or disagree with this statement? Explain your opinion.

3. Do you ever buy things on the Internet? What kinds of things do you buy online? Is this better than shopping in a store? Why or why not?

GO TO MyEnglishLab *TO GIVE YOUR OPINION ABOUT ANOTHER QUESTION.*

COMPREHENSION

🎧 Listen to Professor Chandler's lecture. Read the sentences. Write **T** (true) or **F** (false). Correct the false sentences.

Professor Jason Chandler

_____ 1. KK's experience is useful for business students.

_____ 2. KK made something that many people needed.

_____ 3. KK listened only to her mother.

_____ 4. Adults think it's OK to make mistakes.

_____ 5. If you want to be creative, don't be afraid to make mistakes.

_____ 6. A relaxation exercise can help the students remember their childhood.

_____ 7. The students will remember a time when they were afraid.

VOCABULARY

1 Work with a partner. Student A, read the first sentence. Student B, complete the second sentence with the word or phrase from the box so your sentence has the same meaning. Then switch roles.

came up with	for the first time	made you feel good
completely new	increase their creativity	

1. **STUDENT A:** KK **thought of** a new idea—to make Wristies.

   STUDENT B: That means she _____ the idea to make Wristies.

2. **STUDENT A:** KK started a business, **but she had absolutely no business experience**.

   STUDENT B: So, starting a business was a _____ experience for her.

3. **STUDENT A:**   People can learn to **become more creative**.

   STUDENT B: That means they can _____.

4. **STUDENT A:**   When KK was 17, she spoke at a business school. **She never did that before**.

   STUDENT B: So, when she was 17, she spoke at a business school _____.

5. **STUDENT A:**   When people liked my new idea, it **gave me a happy feeling**.

   STUDENT B: OK, so in other words, it _____

2 🎧 Listen again to Professor Chandler and follow his directions for the relaxation exercise. When you are finished, tell your story to a partner. Then discuss your stories with the class.

■■■■■■■■■■■■■■■■■■■■■■■■■■■■■■■■■■■■GO TO MyEnglishLab *FOR MORE VOCABULARY PRACTICE.*

LISTENING SKILL

LISTENING FOR SIGNAL WORDS FOR MAIN IDEAS

University lectures often follow the pattern Professor Chandler uses:

- divide all the information into clear parts
- use a signal word to begin each new part (each part is a new main idea)

A good listener understands signal words. These important words help listeners to understand what kind of information they will hear next. Some signal words introduce **main ideas**. When you hear the signal word for a **main idea**, you will know that the speaker is going to say something important. Some examples of these signal words are: *first, second, next*. What other signal words do you know?

Try to notice signal words when you listen to a lecture. They will help you to understand how the information in the lecture is organized. After a signal word, you will usually hear a new main idea and then some examples.

🎧 Read the questions and the outline. Then listen to the beginning of Professor Chandler's lecture and fill in the missing information.

1. Professor Chandler wants his students to understand that KK became successful

   because she did _____ important things.
   _(how many?)

(continued on next page)

2. How did Professor Chandler organize the information about what KK did?

Signal Words:

a. _First_

b. _____

c. _____

Main Ideas:

a. _KK had a creative idea._

b. _____

c. _____

■■ *GO TO* MyEnglishLab *FOR MORE SKILL PRACTICE.*

CONNECT THE LISTENINGS

STEP 1: Organize

Professor Chandler told his students that KK had three important lessons to teach them.

1. Find something that people need.

2. Listen to other people.

3. Don't be afraid to do something new.

Look at KK's story. Decide which lesson business students can learn from sentences a–f. Write 1, 2, or 3 in the blank. Sometimes there is more than one lesson.

KK'S STORY

a. KK was wearing gloves, but her wrists were very cold. That's when she had an idea. _____

b. Her friends wore their Wristies every day. They liked them a lot. _____

c. KK's friends told her, "You can sell your Wristies."_____

d. KK's mother had no business experience, but she thought a business was a great idea. _____

e. KK and her mother talked to a lot of people, asked a lot of questions, and learned a lot.

   _____

f. KK went on a TV shopping show to sell Wristies. She was nervous, but it was very exciting.

   She sold 6,000 pairs of Wristies. _____

Nathan, a student in Professor Chandler's business class, took notes during class, but he made some mistakes. After class, he speaks to another student to check his information.

Role-play with a partner. Student A, you're Nathan. Read the notes on the tablet to your classmate. Student B, you're Nathan's classmate. Correct Nathan's mistakes. Then explain what lesson we can learn from KK's experience. Complete the conversation with information from Step 1: Organize. Change roles after sentence 3.

Guest speaker: KK Gregory

1. KK got the idea for Wristies because her fingers were cold.
2. Her friends didn't wear their Wristies.
3. KK's mother said, "Sell your Wristies."
4. KK's mother had a lot of business experience.
5. KK talked to one or two people. She didn't learn a lot.
6. KK sold 600 pairs of Wristies on a TV shopping show.

Example

NATHAN: Well, KK got the idea for Wristies because her **fingers** were cold, right?

CLASSMATE: No, KK was wearing gloves, so her **fingers** were **not** cold. Her **wrists** were cold, and she needed something to make them warm. So, we learn that to have a successful business, you have to find something that people need.

GO TO MyEnglishLab TO CHECK WHAT YOU LEARNED.

VOCABULARY

REVIEW

Work in pairs. Read the story about another young and creative business owner, Brent Simmons. Complete the sentences with words from the box. Then take turns reading the paragraphs aloud.

advice	completely	exciting	increases	made mistakes
afraid to	creative	experience	makes me feel (+ adj.)	owner
came up with	employees	for the first time		successful

Brent Simmons, "Computer Doc"

When Brent Simmons was 10 years old, he knew everything about computers. Whenever

his friends or relatives had problems with their computers, they came to Brent to ask for

his ___advice___. Sometimes, computer store _____ said, "It's
　　　　　1.　　　　　　　　　　　　　　　　　　　　　　2.

impossible to fix this computer. It is _____ broken." But Brent was never
　　　　　　　　　　　　　　　　　　3.

_____ look for a new way to fix it. Sometimes he _____,
　　　4.　　　　　　　　　　　　　　　　　　　　　　　　　　　　5.

and he had to start again. But in the end, he usually _____ a new, very
　　　　　　　　　　　　　　　　　　　　　　　　　　　6.

_____ way to fix the computer.
　　7.

Brent loved to fix computers, and he had a lot of _____. So, when he was

8.

14, he started his own business. Brent is the _____ of the "Computer Doc"

9.

company. When people meet Brent _____, they often think, "He's just a kid.

10.

He can't fix my computer." But after they see his work, they are surprised.

Now Brent is 18 years old. He made more than $50,000 a year when he was in high

school, and the number of people he helps _____ every year. His business is

11.

very _____. But Brent doesn't do this work just to make money. Brent says, "It's

12.

_____ to do work that I love and to help people, too. Sometimes people come

13.

to me with very difficult computer problems. When I can find the problem and fix it, they are

so happy. Helping people with their computer problems _____ great.

14.

EXPAND

🎧 Read and listen to the paragraph about creativity and stress.

When people feel **stressed out**, they can't be creative. So some companies help their
employees to **reduce** their stress. They have free massages and yoga and exercise classes at
work. These **perks** make employees feel **relaxed**, so they can be more creative in their work.
Most employees enjoy these perks a lot. They also **save money** because everything is free,
and they **save time** because they don't need to leave work. These are just a few of the **unusual**
ways that creative companies are increasing their employees' creativity.

(continued on next page)

Work with a partner. Student A, read a sentence in the left column. Student B, read the correct response from the right column. Switch roles for Conversation 2.

CONVERSATION 1: The *Creative Ideas* Company

1. The *Creative Ideas* Company has yoga classes at work.

2. The yoga and exercise classes are free for all employees.

3. Employees at *Creative Ideas* say that they never feel **stressed out** at work.

a. That's a nice **perk**. It helps them to **save money**.

b. That's a great way to **reduce** their employees' stress.

c. That's great. When employees feel **relaxed**, they can be more creative.

CONVERSATION 2: The *Imagine Ads* Company

4. Listen to this. The employees at *Imagine Ads* get three free meals a day, free haircuts, and free car washes!

5. Yeah, but these **perks** really help the employees.

6. The owner of *Imagine Ads* wants everyone to have fun and feel **relaxed** at work.

d. True. They help them to **save time and money**.

e. He understands that you can't be creative when you feel **stressed out**.

f. Wow! Those are **unusual perks** to give employees.

CREATE

Interview two classmates with the following questions. When it is your turn to answer the questions, use the words from Vocabulary Exercises 1 and 2.

1. When do you usually feel **stressed out**? How do you try to **reduce** your stress? Does it always help?

2. In your opinion, is it always good for **employees** to feel **relaxed** at work?

3. Do you know a **successful** business **owner**? How did he or she become **successful**?

4. Are you ever **afraid** to **make a mistake**? In what situations? Why?

5. "Great ideas sometimes come from mistakes." Do you agree with this statement? Explain why or why not.

6. Did you ever solve a problem in a **creative** way? How did you **come up with** the **creative** idea?

7. In the last year, did you do anything **for the first time**? What did you do? How did you feel?

8. In your opinion, what's more important to be **successful**: work **experience** or **creativity**?

■■■■■■■■■■■■■■■■■■■■■■■■■■■■■■ *GO TO* MyEnglishLab *FOR MORE VOCABULARY PRACTICE.*

GRAMMAR

1 Read the conversation. Follow the directions.

PROFESSOR CHANDLER:	Are there any more questions?
STUDENT:	Yes. Were there any problems in the beginning?
KK:	Yeah, there were a few problems. For example, business was very slow at first because there weren't any other people in my company. There was only one person—me! Now there are three employees.

1. Find and underline *there are*, *there was*, *there were*, and *there weren't* in the conversation.

2. Which ones talk about the present? Which ones talk about the past? Which one is singular?

3. Find and underline *Are there* and *Were there*.

THERE IS / THERE ARE, THERE WAS / THERE WERE

1. Use *there is* or *there are* to describe a situation in the present.

There is + *a* + singular count noun	**There is** a website.
There is + non-count noun	**There is** information about Wristies on the website.
Use the contraction *There's* in speaking or informal writing.	**There's** a website. **There's** information about Wristies on the website.
There are + plural count noun	**There are** many places where you can wear Wristies.

(continued on next page)

2. Use **there was** or **there were** to describe a situation in the past.

There was + *a* + singular count noun	**There was** a problem in the beginning.
There was + non-count noun	**There was** snow on the ground.
There were + plural count noun	**There were** problems in the beginning.

3. To form a negative statement, add the contraction **n't**.

There is**n't** any snow.

There are**n't** any more questions.

There were**n't** many employees.

4. For questions, put **is/are** or **was/were** before **there**.

Are there any questions?

Was there a problem yesterday?

When **was there** a problem?

In **yes / no** questions, use **a** with singular nouns, and **any** with plural nouns and non-count nouns.

Is there a problem?

Were there any problems?

Was there any snow?

---

2 Read the interview with Alan Russovich, founder of the Playtime Company. Fill in the blanks using **there** + a form of the verb **be**. Use the contraction **there's** when possible.

Alan: Welcome to Playtime! Please come in.

Interviewer: Wow! This office is very unusual.

Alan: Yes, when people come to our office for the first time, they're usually surprised.

Interviewer: Is this your meeting room?

Alan: No, _____ any meeting rooms at Playtime. This is a
1. (neg.)
"playroom."

Interviewer: A playroom?

Alan: Sure. We learn to be creative from children, and children play.

So this playroom is where we come up with all our new ideas.

_____ a meeting in this playroom one hour ago. Let's look
2.
around.

Interviewer: But . . . _____ any tables or chairs in this room.
3. (neg.)

_____ really a business meeting here? Are you sure? It
4.

looks like children were playing here. _____ balls and
5.

children's toys on the floor, and _____ pictures and pieces
6.

of paper on the floor and walls.

Alan: Those are some ways that we try to increase our creativity. Boring

meetings give people boring ideas. Playtime meetings are exciting!

In Playtime meetings, the employees play. And _____ a
7. (neg.)

table in the room because we don't need one. We write our ideas on

special material on the walls. Do you see that? _____ a
8.

special camera in each playroom. The camera photographs everything

that we write on the walls. OK, now look over there. On that wall,

_____ a list of all the new ideas from the meeting. Let's
9.

see . . . _____ ten people in this room for one hour, and
10.

now _____ 50 new ideas on this list.
11.

Interviewer: This is really an unusual place to work.

Alan: Yeah. Working here is fun, and we're also very successful!

3 Now read the interview aloud with a partner. Switch roles and read it again.

GO TO MyEnglishLab FOR MORE GRAMMAR PRACTICE.

PRONUNCIATION

PRONOUNCING *TH* SOUNDS

Put the tip of your tongue between your teeth.

This is the most important part of the pronunciation of the "th" sound.

Blow out air to make the sound. Be careful: Keep the tip of your
tongue between your teeth while you blow out the air.

The "th" sound in *they, them, there, then, these,* and *mother* is a voiced sound. The vocal cords
vibrate.

The "th" sound in *thumb, thought, things, anything, think,* and *thousand* is a voiceless sound.
The vocal cords do not vibrate.

The tip of the tongue is between the teeth for both sounds.

1 ⊙ Underline every word that has a "th" sound. Then read the sentences aloud to
a partner. Be sure to pronounce all the "th" sounds correctly. Then listen to the
sentences to check your pronunciation.

1. They're long gloves with no fingers.

2. There's a hole for the thumb.

3. Some people wear them outside; others wear them inside.

4. They all wore them every day.

5. So then I thought, "I can sell these things!"

6. My mother didn't know anything about business.

7. A lot of stores sell them, and there's also a website.

2 Work with a partner. Student A, ask the first question. Student B, answer the
question using a word from the box. Student A, listen to your partner's answer. Say,
"That's right" or "I don't think that's right." If you don't think it's right, discuss why.
Take turns being A and B.

anything	thinks	~~thousand~~
mother	thought	thumb

Example

A: How many Wristies did KK sell on TV?

B: She sold six _____thousand_____!

A: _____That's right_____.

1. **A:** Why does KK like business?

   B: She _____ it's exciting.

   A: _____

2. **A:** Who helped KK a lot?

   B: Her _____mother_____ did.

   A: _____

3. **A:** Did KK know a lot about business when she was 10?

   B: No, she didn't know _____anything_____!

   A: _____

4. **A:** Did KK's mother like the idea of selling Wristies?

   B: Yes, she _____ it was a good idea.

   A: _____

5. **A:** Why do Wristies have a little hole?

   B: That's for the _____thumb_____.

   A: _____

SPEAKING SKILL

REACTING TO INFORMATION

When people tell us new information, we usually show our interest. The expression we use depends on whether the news is very surprising or not.

REACTING TO INTERESTING / GENERAL INFORMATION (not surprising)

	KK: And that's how I made the first pair of Wristies.
That's (so) interesting.	**PROF. CHANDLER:** *That's so interesting.*
Uh-huh . . .	**KK:** So, I asked my mother about it, and she thought it was a great idea. And she helped me to start my company.
Really . . . (*falling intonation*)	**PROF. CHANDLER:** *Really . . .*

REACTING TO SURPRISING / UNUSUAL INFORMATION

Wow!	**KK:** I'm 17 now, but when I started my company, I was 10.
That's amazing! / incredible! / unbelievable!	**STUDENT:** *Wow! That's unbelievable!*
Really?! (*rising intonation*)	**KK:** I sold six thousand pairs of Wristies in 6 minutes!
That's great! / wonderful!	**STUDENT:** *That's great!*

Practice reading the reactions in the chart above. Then role-play the conversation about Google's World Headquarters with a partner. Student A, read the sentence. Student B, respond with the best expression from the chart. Take turns being A and B. Try to use all of the expressions.

1. A: Did you know that Google employees can wear jeans to work?

    B: _____

2. **A:** Listen to this! There is a real dinosaur skeleton[1] on the first floor of Google's office!

   B: _____

3. **A:** Google employees play roller hockey[2] twice a week in the parking lot.

   B: _____

4. **A:** Did you know that Google employees can bring their dogs to work?

   B: _____

5. **A:** Google bought its building in California for $319 million.

   B: _____

6. **A:** There are giant red and blue rubber balls all over Google's office.

   B: _____

7. **A:** At Google, three or four employees work together in one space with no walls.

   B: _____

8. **A:** In the Google office, there's an exercise room that is open 24 hours a day.

   B: _____

---

[1] **skeleton:** all the bones in an animal or person

[2] **roller hockey:** a sport played on the street; players use long curved sticks to hit a ball into a goal; the players wear Rollerblades®

■ ■ ■ ■ ■ ■ ■ ■ ■ ■ ■ ■ *GO TO* MyEnglishLab *FOR MORE SKILL PRACTICE AND TO CHECK WHAT YOU LEARNED.*

FINAL SPEAKING TASK

A role play is a short performance. The students take on roles, or become characters, and act out a situation.

You are going to role-play a business meeting at Google. Google wants to build a new office in Philadelphia, Pennsylvania. The company wants to help its employees to be more creative. Today, office designers are meeting with employees from Google's California and New York offices. The designers want to know which ideas from each office they should use in the new Philadelphia office. You will play the role of a designer or a Google employee. Use the vocabulary, grammar, pronunciation, and language for reacting to information from this unit.*

STEP 1: Form three large groups: (1) office designers, (2) employees from Googleplex, Google's California office, and (3) employees from Googleplex East, Google's New York office.

STEP 2: Prepare for the role play.

- **Office designers:** Prepare at least 10 questions to ask the Google employees from the California and New York offices.

Examples

Is there anything unusual in your office?   Do the employees usually feel relaxed at work?

Are there any yoga or exercise rooms?   How many cafeterias or restaurants are there?

- **Employees from Googleplex, California:** Read the information about your office. Decide which ideas are **the most important for creativity**.

GOOGLEPLEX, CALIFORNIA

an indoor rock climbing wall (for exercise)	ten cafeterias
an outdoor sand volleyball court	an exercise room
two lap-swimming pools	a game room
car washes	a four-star restaurant
glass walls between the offices inside	a hair salon
a video game room	a sushi bar
a massage room	a doctor's office
funny posters on the walls	

PERKS

free chef-prepared food all day

free massages

skateboards

free sports training

free bus from employees' homes to work

---

* For Alternative Speaking Topics, see page 109.

- **Employees from Googleplex East, New York:** Read the information about your office. Decide which ideas are **the most important for creativity**.

GOOGLEPLEX EAST, NEW YORK

glass walls between the offices inside

big red rubber exercise balls

balloons with happy faces all around the building

a game room with foosball, air hockey, a billiards table

whiteboards on the walls—employees can write any ideas they have, and other employees can add their ideas

Razor® scooters

electric train sets

massage chairs

a dog play area

PERKS
free chair massages
employees' dogs (but not cats) can come to work with them

STEP 3: Form small groups with one student from each of the large groups. Now each group has at least one *office designer*, one *employee from Googleplex, CA,* and one *employee from Googleplex East, NY.*

STEP 4: Each group will discuss and choose which ideas to use for the new Google office. Office designers, ask all of your questions. You can begin the meeting like this:

DESIGNER: Tell me about *Googleplex* in California. Is there anything unusual in it?

CALIFORNIA: Well, there is a massage room for all the employees.

DESIGNER: Really?

CALIFORNIA: Yes. So when employees feel stressed out, they can . . .

DESIGNER: And does that really help to increase their creativity?

CALIFORNIA: Sure! When employees feel stressed out, they can't come up with . . .

NEW YORK: I agree completely. We don't have a massage room in the New York office, but there are . . .

DESIGNER: OK, so massages are important.

STEP 5: Each group will write the ideas it chose on the board or on a large piece of paper. Then, as a class, select the ideas and perks that both groups agreed on for the new Google office in Philadelphia. Explain why those ideas are the best ways to increase creativity.

UNIT PROJECT

Find out about a young business owner or entrepreneur (18 years old or younger).

STEP 1: Look on the Internet, in the library, or in business magazines, or tell about a person you know. If you use the Internet, search for the key words "young entrepreneurs."

STEP 2: Research the person and his/her idea. Here are some questions to guide your research:

- What was the person's idea?

- How old was the person when he/she thought of the idea?

- Did it work the first time?

- Did he/she get help from anyone?

- What does the person do now?

STEP 3: Prepare a short oral report. Share your information with the class.

Listening Task

Listen to your classmates' presentations, react to any interesting or surprising information, and ask questions. Try to use some of the new language from this unit.

ALTERNATIVE SPEAKING TOPICS

Many companies want their employees to be more creative. These companies have unusual activities for employees. Here are some of the activities. Which are good ways to increase creativity? Which are not? Check (✓) the boxes. Then explain your reasons to a small group of classmates.

	IT'S A GOOD IDEA.	IT'S NOT A GOOD IDEA.	I'M NOT SURE.
Doing exciting outdoor sports together (rock climbing, whitewater rafting, etc.)			
Studying music (alone or with co-workers)			
Sometimes working at home			
Learning how to meditate or do yoga			
Playing with children's toys (electric trains, giant rubber balls, air hockey, etc.)			
Writing new ideas on the walls			
Getting a massage during work time			
Exercising in the gym during work time			

GO TO MyEnglishLab *TO DISCUSS ONE OF THE ALTERNATIVE TOPICS, WATCH A VIDEO ABOUT SELLING HOT DOGS, AND TAKE THE UNIT 4 ACHIEVEMENT TEST.*

UNDERSTANDING FEARS AND Phobias

1 FOCUS ON THE TOPIC

1. Look at the photo. Why are some people scared[1] of snakes?

2. Why are some people scared of certain things?

3. Does having a fear of something change a person's life? How?

---

[1] **scared:** afraid or frightened; having a fear

GO TO MyEnglishLab *TO CHECK WHAT YOU KNOW.*

2 FOCUS ON LISTENING

VOCABULARY

1 🎧 A phobia is a very strong fear. Read and listen to the blog about arachnophobia, the fear of spiders.

PHOBIAS: You Are Not Alone

HOME

COMMENT

ABOUT US

(June 9) Arachnophobia

There are many different kinds of phobias. One is arachnophobia, the **fear** of spiders. People with arachnophobia are very scared of spiders. Their hearts beat fast when they see a spider, and sometimes they cry or **shake**. Other people laugh at them. They say, "Why are you so afraid of a little spider?" But remember—many people have this problem. Having arachnophobia is **not your fault**.

(June 12) Comments

(1) Thanks for explaining this. I am very scared of spiders. Sometimes I can't sleep at night because I worry about spiders in my house. My friends say that I'm really not **in danger**, but spiders are **still** a big problem for me. I feel like they're going to kill me! (**Just kidding.**)

—Jenn

(2) I worry about spiders, too. This is **a serious issue** in my life. Do you know that some spiders can **hurt** you? That's why I look for them in my house. And I worry about spiders outside the house, too. Spiders are everywhere. You can't always see them—but they're there. I don't know what to do. I'm **confused** about this, and sometimes I**'m angry with** myself.

—Deepa

2 Match the words and phrases on the left with the definitions on the right. Write the letter of the correct definition on the line.

_____ 1. a serious issue   **a.** you didn't make a problem happen

_____ 2. be angry with   **b.** I'm joking; I'm not serious.

_____ 3. confused   **c.** in a situation that may hurt or kill you

_____ 4. fear   **d.** move back and forth quickly

_____ 5. hurt   **e.** feel mad or upset because something is not OK

_____ 6. in danger   **f.** up to now

_____ 7. not your fault   **g.** make a person feel pain

_____ 8. just kidding   **h.** not understanding

_____ 9. shake   **i.** feeling of being in danger

_____ 10. still   **j.** a big problem

■■■■■■■■■■■■■■■■■■■■■■■■■■■■■GO TO MyEnglishLab *FOR MORE VOCABULARY PRACTICE.*

PREVIEW

You are listening to *Psyched*, a call-in radio show. The host of the show is Doctor Jones. She is a psychologist, someone who helps people understand their feelings.

🎧 Listen to the excerpt from *Psyched: A Radio Show*. Then answer the questions. Discuss your answers with the class.

1. According to Doctor Jones, what is a phobia? (Circle one.)

   a. a shaking body

   b. a real danger

   c. a strong fear

2. What happens to people with phobias? (Circle one.)

   a. They feel like they are in danger.

   b. They are in danger.

   c. They feel very strong.

3. What words will you probably hear in this radio show? (Check (✓) three.)

   _____ afraid

   _____ happy

   _____ scared

   _____ problem

   _____ money

   _____ serious

MAIN IDEAS

1 🎧 Listen to the whole show. Look at the answers you predicted in the Preview section on page 113. Did your predictions help you to understand the radio show?

2 Choose the best answer to each question.

1. What does Doctor Jones say about phobias?

   _____ **a.** A phobia can't hurt you.

   _____ **b.** A phobia changes your life.

2. What happened to Anna because of her phobia?

_____ **a.** She was excited in Paris.

_____ **b.** She was scared in Paris.

3. What is Anna's advice about phobias?

_____ **a.** Don't be angry with yourself.

_____ **b.** Don't take a job for a million dollars.

4. Why is Anna's life better today?

_____ **a.** She can ride elevators.

_____ **b.** She reads many books.

DETAILS

Listen again. Write **T** (true) or **F** (false). Correct the false information.

_____ **1.** Arachnophobia is the fear of spiders.

_____ **2.** People with phobias sometimes shake.

_____ **3.** A phobia is being afraid of danger.

_____ **4.** Claustrophobia is the fear of small spaces.

_____ **5.** Anna cared about the kids in the Eiffel Tower.

_____ **6.** Anna was scared of elevators and cars.

_____ **7.** Writing helps Anna feel less afraid.

_____ **8.** Anna's life is easy today.

_____ **9.** Having a phobia is your fault.

_____ **10.** Many people have phobias.

GO TO MyEnglishLab FOR MORE LISTENING PRACTICE.

MAKE INFERENCES

UNDERSTANDING THE MEANING OF EXAGGERATIONS

An inference is a guess about something that is not directly stated. To make an inference, use information that you understand from what you hear.

Speakers sometimes use exaggerations, or impossible words or phrases, to help make a point. Exaggerations are impossible statements because they describe things that are bigger than things in real life. Speakers use exaggerations to make ideas sound more interesting.

🎧 Listen to the example. Answer the question.

Example

The speaker says she "was going to die." What does this mean? Look at the following choices:

    a. She could die inside the Eiffel Tower.

    b. She felt very afraid inside the Eiffel Tower.

The answer is: **b.** Usually, people do not die when they go inside high towers. This is an exaggeration, or impossible statement. The meaning of the exaggeration is that the person had a very strong fear of high places. She *felt* like she was going to die when she was inside the Eiffel Tower. She wasn't really going to die, but she felt that way because her fear was very strong.

🎧 Listen to the excerpts. Think about the exaggeration. What do you think the speaker is really trying to say?

Excerpt One

Why does the speaker use the word *forever*?

_____ **a.** She spent a long time climbing stairs.

_____ **b.** She wasted time because of her phobia.

Excerpt Two

Why does the speaker use the phrase "twenty books a week"?

_____ **a.** She reads many books.

_____ **b.** She is a very good reader.

Why does the speaker use the phrase "a million dollars"?

_____ **a.** People with elevator phobias can lose important chances.

_____ **b.** It costs a lot of money to have an elevator phobia.

EXPRESS OPINIONS

Discuss the questions with a partner.

1. What do you think about the Eiffel Tower story? Do you sometimes get scared in high buildings?

2. Do you have a phobia? Do you know someone with a phobia? Explain.

3. Do you think books and doctors can help people with phobias? What other things can help? Explain.

■■■■■■■■■■■■■■■■■■ *GO TO* MyEnglishLab *TO GIVE YOUR OPINION ABOUT ANOTHER QUESTION.*

COMPREHENSION

Driving across a bridge is very difficult for people with bridge and driving phobias. In this listening, Allen is a man with these problems. He is driving across a bridge with the help of a psychologist.

🎧 **Listen to the conversation between Allen and the psychologist. Then circle the correct answer to complete each sentence.**

1. Allen is afraid _____.

   a. a truck will hit him

   b. of driving a truck

2. The psychologist tells him to think of other things _____.

   a. that he is afraid of

   b. that he does well

3. The psychologist tells him to _____.

   a. look straight ahead

   b. look at the trucks

4. In the end, Allen feels _____.

   a. very happy that he crossed the bridge

   b. unhappy because he didn't cross the bridge alone

VOCABULARY

Read the conversation and notice the phrases in bold. Match the phrases on the left to the definitions on the right. Write the letter of the correct definition on the line.

YOUNG MAN: I can't ride this bike! I'm going to fall!

FRIEND: **Calm down.** You can do it.

YOUNG MAN: I don't know how. **What's wrong with me?**

FRIEND: **Come on,** you can do it. You need to **believe in yourself.**

YOUNG MAN: How can I do that? I'm going to fall!

FRIEND: Just **keep going.** Don't **give up.**

_____ 1. believe in yourself   a. why do I have this problem?

_____ 2. calm down   b. don't stop doing something

_____ 3. come on   c. stop feeling scared

_____ 4. keep going   d. have a good opinion of yourself

_____ 5. what's wrong with me?   e. stop trying

_____ 6. give up   f. something we say to help others feel stronger

■■■■■■■■■■■■■■■■■■■■■■■■■■■■ *GO TO* MyEnglishLab *FOR MORE VOCABULARY PRACTICE.*

LISTENING SKILL

NOTICING CONTRADICTIONS

When speakers disagree with each other, they sometimes contradict the other speaker. To contradict, you say the opposite of what the other person says.

🎧 Listen to the example.

Example

Who is disagreeing with whom? How do we know?

In this example, the psychologist is disagreeing with Allen. He is saying the opposite of what Allen says. We know this because he puts stress on the word *not* to make the meaning clear. This contradiction shows that the psychologist disagrees with Allen about the trucks.

🎧 Listen to two excerpts from "Crossing a Bridge." Pay attention to contradictions. Who is disagreeing with whom? What are the two speakers disagreeing about? Which words do they put stress on?

Excerpt One

Who is disagreeing with whom? How do we know?

a. Allen disagrees with the psychologist.

b. The psychologist disagrees with Allen.

How do we know? He stresses the word _____.

Excerpt Two

Who is disagreeing with whom?

a. Allen disagrees with the psychologist.

b. The psychologist disagrees with Allen.

How do we know? He stresses the word _____.

■■■■■■■■■■■■■■■■■■■■■■■■■■■■■■■■■■ *GO TO* MyEnglishLab *FOR MORE SKILL PRACTICE.*

STEP 1: Organize

Look at the chart. Work with a partner to complete the chart with information from Listening One and Listening Two.

	TYPE OF PHOBIA	WHERE THEY GOT HELP	HOW THEY FEEL ABOUT PHOBIAS
ANNA	a. fear of _small places_ b. fear of high places	a. books b. _Doctors_	a. A phobia is a _____. b. Don't be _____. c. Does she feel OK? (Circle one.) Yes / No
ALLEN	a. fear of bridges b. fear of _____	a. _____ b. doctors	a. He _is scared_ crossing bridges. b. He feels that something is "wrong" with him. c. Does he feel OK? (Circle one.) Yes / No

STEP 2: Synthesize

Work in groups of three to create an interview. Student A, you are Anna. Student B, you are Allen. Student C, you are a reporter. Complete the interview with information from the chart in Step 1: Organize. Then read the conversation aloud.

REPORTER: What kind of phobias do you have?

ANNA: I have _____. This means _____.

ALLEN: I have the same problem. I can't _____.

REPORTER: Does anything help you with this?

ANNA: Yes! I think _____.

ALLEN: I disagree. I don't think _____.

REPORTER: Tell me more—How do you feel about having a phobia?

ALLEN: I feel _____.

ANNA: Not me. I feel _____.

■■ *GO TO* MyEnglishLab *TO CHECK WHAT YOU LEARNED.*

3 FOCUS ON SPEAKING

VOCABULARY

REVIEW

A psychologist is speaking to a young person. This young person is worried about having a phobia. Read the conversation and fill in the blanks with the words from the box. You will not use all of the words.

calm down	in danger
come on	issue
confused	shake
fear	still
hurt	wrong with

·Dr. Jones, Psychologist·
In Session

PSYCHOLOGIST: So, why are you here today? How can I help?

YOUNG MAN: Well, I'm 25 years old, and some of my friends are getting married. I have a girlfriend, but when I think about getting married, I get a really strong feeling of _____. Do you
1.
think I have a phobia?

PSYCHOLOGIST: I don't think so. Many people feel scared about getting married.

YOUNG MAN: Really? Are you sure I don't have a phobia? How do you know?

PSYCHOLOGIST: First of all, people with phobias feel like they are _____
2.
when they are not. There's really no reason to be scared. But you have a good reason. I think you're scared because you're not ready to get married.

YOUNG MAN: But my friends are ready. They're getting married. What's

_____ me? Why am I so scared? Am I just a big baby?
3.

PSYCHOLOGIST: _____ . Don't be angry with yourself. This is a/an
4.

_____ for many people—not feeling ready to get married.
5.

YOUNG MAN: Maybe you're right. But when I think about getting married, my heart

beats fast and my hands _____ . My whole body feels bad.
6.

Are you sure I don't have a phobia?

PSYCHOLOGIST: I'm sure you don't. There are good reasons to feel scared of getting

married.

YOUNG MAN: What are they?

PSYCHOLOGIST: Well, first of all, marriage is not easy. Married people sometimes fight

and _____ each other. Sometimes they're very unhappy.
7.

This is a big decision. Don't get married if you're not sure about it. Don't

do it if you feel _____ .
8.

YOUNG MAN: But what if I never get married? What about my parents? They really

want me to get married, but I'm _____ not sure. My
9.

parents will be so angry!

PSYCHOLOGIST: Please, _____ . Don't get so upset. When you are ready to
10.

get married, you'll know it. You'll be happy, not scared.

EXPAND

1 Read the advertisement for an e-book, *Power of Speaking in Public*.[2] Notice the words in bold.

Do you know the #1 fear of Americans? Speaking in public! Are you afraid of speaking in public? You are not alone. This is a very **common** problem. You can **deal with** your fear today. You can become more **confident**. Our e-book, *Power of Speaking in Public*, will really give you **power**. You will speak better and better. You will lose all your fear of speaking in front of others. Try *Power of Speaking in Public*!

_____

[2] **speaking in public:** speaking in front of a large group of people

2 Complete the sentences by matching each sentence beginning on the left with the correct ending on the right. Write the letter of the correct ending on the line.

_____ 1. If a problem is **common** . . .   **a.** you find a way to solve it.

_____ 2. When you **deal with** a problem . . .   **b.** believe they can do things.

_____ 3. **Confident** people . . .   **c.** you can change a situation.

_____ 4. If you have **power** . . .   **d.** many people have it.

CREATE

Look at the list of fears. Discuss the questions with a partner. Use words from Review and Expand.

- elevators
- dogs
- insects
- darkness
- public speaking
- driving

1. What kind of issues do people with these fears have?

2. What's the best way to deal with these fears?

3. Which one of these fears do you think is common? Why?

■■■■■■■■■■■■■■■■■■■■■■■■■■■■■■ *GO TO* MyEnglishLab *FOR MORE VOCABULARY PRACTICE.*

GRAMMAR

1 Read the excerpts. Then answer the questions.

> **ANNA:** I always walked up the stairs—and it took forever!
>
> **PSYCHOLOGIST:** There! You did it! You crossed the bridge!
>
> **ALLEN:** *We* crossed the bridge.

1. What are the verbs? Underline them.

2. How are the verbs similar? How are they different?

SIMPLE PAST	
Use the simple past to describe finished actions or situations.	
1. We use the simple past to talk about a specific time in the past: *last year, last month, yesterday,* and so on.	Anna **climbed** the stairs last year.
2. Some simple past verbs are regular. Add **-ed** to the verbs (*walked, wanted*).	Allen **walked** to work. He **wanted** to stay away from cars.
3. Some simple past verbs are irregular (*got, became*).	Allen **got** scared of the trucks. Anna's life **became** easier.
4. To make the negative form of the simple past, use **_didn't_** plus the base form of the verb.	Anna **didn't take** the elevator. Allen **didn't cross** the bridge alone.

2 Read the information about the fear of clowns. Complete the sentences with the simple past tense of each verb. Then work with a partner. Take turns reading each sentence aloud.

(continued on next page)

THE FEAR OF CLOWNS

Many children and adults react with fear to clowns. A few years ago, British psychologists

_____ the reaction of more than 250 children. They _____
    1. (study)   2. (ask)

the children about pictures of clowns in a children's hospital. All the children

_____ strong fear. They _____ that the clown pictures
    3. (show)   4. (say)

_____ scary. Also, in the 1990s, many adults _____ scared
    5. (be)   6. (get)

when they _____ the movie *It*. In this movie, a clown _____
              7. (watch)   8. (make)

friends and then _____ them. After watching this movie, some people
                9. (hurt)

_____, and their hearts _____ fast. Recently, one doctor in
    10. (cry)   11. (beat)

Canada _____ that clowns are scary because they wear a lot of makeup. In
      12. (explain)

her opinion, people need to see faces. She believes that people have a strong reason to be

afraid of clowns. It is because they cannot see their real faces.

3 Work with a partner to discuss fears that you (or someone else) had in the past. Student A, interview Student B about a fear in the past. Student B, tell your own true story about your fear or the fear of someone you know. Student A, listen and take notes. Then switch roles. Use your notes to prepare a report for the class.

Interview Questions

1. What kind of fear did you (or someone else) have?

2. How old were you (or someone else)?

3. Why did you (or someone else) have this fear?

4. How did you (or the other person) feel? Were you angry or confused?

5. How did this fear change your life?

Example

My partner is Justin. When Justin **was** 10 years old, he **was** very afraid of dogs. He **had** a reason for this fear. One time, a big dog **hurt** his older brother. After this, he started shaking when he **saw** dogs. His heart **beat** faster, and he **cried**. He **stayed** home often. Sometimes, when friends **invited** him to their houses, he **didn't go**. He **didn't want** to see their dogs.

GO TO MyEnglishLab FOR MORE GRAMMAR PRACTICE.

PRONUNCIATION

PAST TENSE: -*ED* ENDINGS

The -*ed* ending is sometimes pronounced as a new syllable and sometimes as a new sound.

🎧 Listen to Allen's explanation of an accident.

Example

ALLEN: The driver in front of me <u>stopped</u> quickly. I don't know why he <u>needed</u> to stop. I <u>tried</u> to stop, too, but it was too late. When I <u>stopped</u>, the driver behind me <u>crashed</u>³ into my car!

Look at the underlined verbs. Is the -*ed* ending a new syllable or a new sound?

_____

³ **crash:** to hit very hard

PRONOUNCING -*ED* ENDINGS

1. If the last sound in the base verb is /d/ or /t/, -*ed* is pronounced as a new syllable: /ɪd/ or /əd/.	/ɪd/ The other driver **wanted** to stop.
2. With other verbs, the -*ed* ending is pronounced as a new sound, not a syllable:	/ɪd/ I **decided** to stop, too.
a. If the last sound in the base verb is /p/, /f/, /k/, /s/, /ʃ/, or /tʃ/, -*ed* is pronounced /t/. (See the phonetic alphabet on p. 236.)	/t/ The car **stopped** quickly.
b. After all other verbs, the -*ed* ending is pronounced /d/. (See the phonetic alphabet on p. x.)	/d/ Allen **explained** the accident. /d/ Allen **changed** his way of driving.

1 🎧 Listen to the words. Circle the correct -**ed** ending.

1. wanted   /t/ /d/ /ɪd/   **5.** walked   /t/ /d/ /ɪd/

2. changed   /t/ /d/ /ɪd/   **6.** decided   /t/ /d/ /ɪd/

3. tried   /t/ /d/ /ɪd/   **7.** stopped   /t/ /d/ /ɪd/

4. needed   /t/ /d/ /ɪd/   **8.** started   /t/ /d/ /ɪd/

2 🎧 Listen to the sentences about Dr. Jones, the psychologist in Listening One. Then repeat each sentence and look at the underlined verbs. Is **-ed** pronounced /t/, /d/, or /ɪd/? Write your answers above the verbs.

/ /
1. She <u>wanted</u> to help others with their problems.

/ /
2. She <u>studied</u> at New York University.

/ /
3. After she <u>graduated</u>, she became a psychologist.

/ /
4. She <u>worked</u> at a hospital for three years.

/ /
5. She <u>talked</u> to many people about their problems.

/ /
6. Then she <u>decided</u> to start a radio show.

/ /
7. She <u>helped</u> many people with fears and phobias.

/ /
8. She also <u>earned</u> a lot of money for her work.

/ /
9. After many years of working, she <u>stopped</u>.

/ /
10. She <u>decided</u> to enjoy life at the beach.

3 Work in groups of three to tell the story of Allen's phobia. Use the past tense of the verb in parentheses to make a complete sentence. One person in the group will start the story and the other members of the group will continue the story. Be careful to pronounce the past tense ending correctly.

Example

When he was a young man, he

a. (start) to be afraid of many things.

The correct response is: When he was a young man, he **started** to be afraid of many things.

1. When he was a young man, he

    a. (stop) driving his car.

    b. (walk) to work every day.

    c. (decide) to see a psychologist.

2. While working with the psychologist, he

    a. (learn) a new way of thinking about himself.

    b. (change) his old ideas about driving.

    c. (try) to cross the bridge in his car.

3. After working with the psychologist, he

    a. (want) to try new things.

    b. (study) planes and flying.

    c. (start) flying a small plane.

SPEAKING SKILL

USING IMPERATIVES

Speakers often use imperatives to give advice. An imperative is the command form of a verb. It is always in present tense. **Don't** is used in the negative form. The subject is "you" since the speaker is giving a command to other people. However, the word *you* is not included in the imperative.

🎧 Listen to the examples from Listening One and Listening Two. Underline the imperative in each one. Then listen again and repeat the imperative verb.

Examples

1. Believe me, a phobia is a very serious issue.

2. Don't be angry with yourself.

3. Think of all the other things you do well.

4. Don't look at the trucks. Just look at the road.

Work with a partner to give each other advice. Use imperatives. Student A, give advice for items 1–3. Student B, give advice for items 4–6.

1. **B:** I'm scared of taking my driving test.

   A: Don't _____. You can do it.

2. **B:** I don't like elevators.

   A: _____ instead!

3. **B:** I get scared when I travel alone.

   A: _____. Then you won't be alone!

4. **A:** I want a pet, but I'm afraid of dogs.

   B: _____. They don't bite.

5. **A:** I don't want to fly to San Francisco from New York.

   B: _____ You'll see more.

6. **A:** I hate that clown movie!

   B: Don't _____. Play a game instead.

■ ■ ■ ■ ■ ■ ■ ■ ■ ■ ■ ■ ■ ■ ■ ■GO TO MyEnglishLab *FOR MORE SKILL PRACTICE AND TO CHECK WHAT YOU LEARNED.*

FINAL SPEAKING TASK

In this task, you will create and perform a 1–3 minute role play about phobias. Try to use the vocabulary, grammar, pronunciation, and language for using imperatives that you learned in this unit.*

Work in pairs. Look at the story strip. Student A, you are a person with a water phobia. Student B, you have the same phobia, but your life is better today. Follow these steps:

STEP 1: Think about the situation. Plan your conversation. Follow these points:

- Student A, explain your problem. Talk about your water phobia and all your problems—all the things you can't do in your life.

- Student B, tell about your life in the past. You had a difficult life with your water phobia. But your life is better today. Give some advice to Student A.

STEP 2: Practice the role play several times. Act like your character and speak naturally. As you practice, write notes about what you will say. Ask your teacher for help as needed.

STEP 3: Perform your role play for the class.

Listening Task

Watch the role plays. Which role play did you like best? Discuss with a partner why you liked that role play.

---

* For Alternative Speaking Topics, see page 132.

UNIT PROJECT

STEP 1: Look at the list of phobias. Use the Internet to learn more about one of them. Be sure to use a website that you can trust. The best websites to use are from the government, universities, or professional organizations.

achluophobia (fear of the dark)	gamophobia (fear of marriage)	scolionophobia (fear of school)
botanophobia (fear of plants)	ombrophobia (fear of rain)	*your own idea*
chrometophobia (fear of money)	papyrophobia (fear of paper)	

Answer these questions about one of the phobias.

1. What is _____?

2. What kind of problems do people with _____ have?

3. What's your advice for people with this phobia? What's your advice for their family and friends?

4. What are some other interesting facts about _____?

STEP 2: Prepare an oral report. Share your answers to the questions in Step 1.

STEP 3: Give your report to the class. Try to answer questions about the phobia.

■■■■■■■■■■■■■■■■■■■■■■■■■■■■■■■■■■GO TO MyEnglishLab *TO PRACTICE INTERNET SKILLS.*

ALTERNATIVE SPEAKING TOPICS

Discuss one of the topics. Use the vocabulary and grammar from the unit.

1. Do you believe that psychologists can really help people with their issues? Why or why not? What are some other ways to help people with their problems in life?

2. Tell the story of someone you know—a person with a serious issue in his or her life. (Serious issues include problems with health, money, fears, or other people.) Is this person happy or unhappy? How does this person deal with his or her issues? What can we learn from this person?

■■■■■■■■■■■■■■■*GO TO* MyEnglishLab *TO DISCUSS ONE OF THE ALTERNATIVE TOPICS, WATCH A VIDEO ABOUT THE WORLD'S WEIRDEST PHOBIAS, AND TAKE THE UNIT 5 ACHIEVEMENT TEST.* ■■■■■■■■■■

RISKS AND
Challenges

1 FOCUS ON THE TOPIC

1. What's happening in this photo? Is it dangerous? What is the swimmer wearing?

2. Have you ever done something very difficult?

3. Have you ever done something that you were afraid to do?

GO TO MyEnglishLab TO CHECK WHAT YOU KNOW.

VOCABULARY

1 Read and listen to the radio documentary about Diana Nyad.

Diana Nyad

DIANA NYAD

Diana Nyad grew up in south Florida, near the ocean. When she was only eight years old, she **decided** to be the first person to swim from Cuba to Florida, a **distance** of 103 miles (166 km). Diana joined her school swim team in fifth grade. After her coach watched her for 15 minutes, he said, "Kid, one day, you're going to be the best swimmer in the world." He was right! Diana Nyad became an **amazing** swimmer, and she **set** many **world records**. From 1969 to 1979, she was the best long-**distance** swimmer in the world.

At age 28, Diana tried to **reach her** childhood **goal** for the first time. She started swimming from Cuba to Florida. **Unfortunately**, after 42 hours, the weather became very bad. There was a lot of rain and wind. Diana saw that it was impossible to reach Florida, so she had to stop. One year later, Diana set a new record. She swam the longest distance of any swimmer (man or woman) in history—102.5 miles (164 km) from the Bahamas to Florida.

Then, Diana Nyad did not swim again for 30 years.

For 30 years, Nyad worked as a TV and radio sports reporter. She was very successful, but as she got older, she wasn't happy. She felt that she

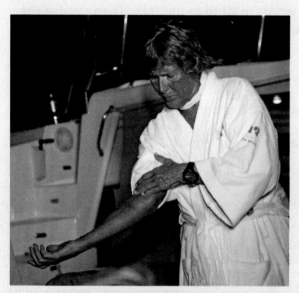

jellyfish bites on Diana Nyad's body

At the age of 60, Diana began the very difficult training. For more than a year, she swam 8 to 14 hours every day. When people asked Diana why she wanted to try the difficult swim again, she just said, "It is never too late to start your dream." The ocean between Cuba and Florida is full of **dangerous** *jellyfish* and *sharks*, but Diana **was determined** to swim **without** a *shark cage* to protect her.

Over the next four years, Diana started the swim from Cuba to Florida three times, but **unfortunately**, each time, the jellyfish bites and very bad weather stopped her. After the fourth time, Diana thought, "Maybe it's impossible to **reach my goal**," but a few days later, she changed her mind. On August 31, 2013, eleven days after her 64th birthday, Diana Nyad jumped into the ocean near Cuba and began to swim to Florida again.

needed a new **challenge** in her life. That's when she started thinking again about her old dream. She decided to swim from Cuba to Florida again.

a jellyfish

swimming inside a shark cage

2 Take turns with a partner. Look at the words in **bold** in the text. Then choose the best meaning. Your partner will tell you if she/he agrees or not. The first one has been done for you.

1. **A:** **Distance** is the amount of (*space* / *time*) between two places or things.

    B: (Yes, I agree. / No, I don't think so. I think it is the amount of . . .)

2. **A:** An **amazing** swimmer means "(*an excellent* / *a good*) swimmer."

    B: (Yes, I agree. / No, I don't think so. I think it means . . .)

3. **A:** She **decided** means "She thought about something and (*made a choice* / *changed her mind*)."

    B: (Yes, I agree. / No, I don't think so. I think it means she . . .)

4. **A:** She **set world records** means "She did things (*all over the world* / *better than any other person in the world*)."

    B: (Yes, I agree. / No, I don't think so. I think it means she . . .)

5. **A:** She tried to **reach her goal** means "She tried to do something that was (*her dream* / *very important*)."

    B: (Yes, I agree. / No, I don't think so. I think it means she . . .)

6. **A:** **Unfortunately** means "This is (*lucky* / *sad*) information."

    B: (Yes, I agree. / No, I don't think so. I think it means this . . .)

7. **A:** A **challenge** is something you enjoy doing because it is (*easy* / *difficult*).

    B: (Yes, I agree. / No, I don't think so. I think it is . . .)

8. **A:** Jellyfish and sharks are **dangerous** because they (*can kill people* / *are in the ocean*).

    B: (Yes, I agree. / No, I don't think so. I think they are dangerous because they . . .)

9. **A:** She **is determined** means "No one (*can stop her* / *is better than she is*)."

    B: (Yes, I agree. / No, I don't think so. I think it means no one . . .)

10. **A:** **Without** a shark cage means "(*outside a shark cage* / *with no shark cage*)."

    B: (Yes, I agree. / No, I don't think so. I think it means . . .)

PREVIEW

(⌒) Two sports reporters are talking about Diana Nyad on the radio. Listen to the beginning of their news report. Check (✓) the things they are going to talk about next.

_____ Diana's world records   _____ sharks

_____ the weather   _____ singing songs

_____ Diana's childhood   _____ Diana's age

_____ jellyfish   _____ life in Cuba

MAIN IDEAS

1 (⌒) Listen to the entire news report. Now look again at your answers in Preview above. Were any of your answers correct? Did they help you to understand the report?

2 (⌒) Listen to the news report again. Choose the best word or phrase to complete each sentence.

1. Diana is having a difficult time because of the (*jellyfish bites / sharks*).

2. Diana feels sick, but she doesn't want to (*go back to Cuba / give up*).

3. Long distance swimming is difficult because the swimmer (*is alone in the water / doesn't have a team of helpers*).

4. To swim long distances, Diana trains her body and her (*mind / breathing*).

5. Diana uses a kind of meditation[1] to help her to (*enjoy swimming more / continue swimming for a very long time*).

6. Diana doesn't give up easily because she enjoys (*setting a record / having a challenge*).

7. Diana is very (*determined / afraid*) to reach her goal.

8. Diana is a great example for many people who want to (*set a new goal in their life / become amazing swimmers*).

---

[1] **meditation:** spending time in quiet thought in order to clear your mind or relax

DETAILS

Listen again. Write **T** (true) or **F** (false). Correct the false information.

_____ 1. Diana is swimming from Cuba to Florida for the fourth time.

_____ 2. Diana started swimming 31 hours ago.

_____ 3. Diana's wetsuit covers her mouth.

_____ 4. Diana is having trouble breathing.

_____ 5. Diana thinks that long-distance swimming is a lonely sport.

_____ 6. Diana clears her mind by counting and singing.

_____ 7. Diana can count to 1,000 in four languages.

_____ 8. Diana thinks long-distance swimming is easier for young people.

GO TO MyEnglishLab FOR MORE LISTENING PRACTICE.

MAKE INFERENCES

UNDERSTANDING RHETORICAL QUESTIONS

An inference is a guess about something that is not directly stated. To make an inference, use information that you understand from what you hear.

People use *rhetorical questions* to show that they have very strong feelings about something. Rhetorical questions are not real questions, so listeners do *not* answer them.

When people ask rhetorical questions, they pronounce the stressed words with *extra strong stress*—much stronger stress than usual. It's important to notice the difference between *real* questions and *rhetorical* questions, so you can understand a speaker's meaning.

Listen to Examples 1 and 2 and answer the questions.

Example 1
What does Jim's question mean?

a. How is Diana able to swim in these terrible conditions?

b. It's amazing that Diana can continue swimming even in these terrible conditions!

The correct answer is: **b.** It's amazing that Diana can continue swimming even in these terrible conditions!

Explanation

This is a rhetorical question. Jim wants to show how strongly he feels that Diana is an amazing swimmer. He uses extra strong stress on the question word *How* and the main verb *do*. Jim does not expect an answer from Sue because this is not a real question. Notice that Sue responds by agreeing with Jim's strong feeling.

Example 2

What does Jim's question mean?

a. How does Diana clear her mind?

b. I can't believe that Diana knows how to completely clear her mind!

The correct answer is: **a.** How does Diana clear her mind?

Explanation

Jim asks the same question as in Example 1, but here he is asking a *real* question, not a *rhetorical* one. He pronounces the question word *How* and the main verb *do* with regular stress. Jim asks this question because he wants Sue to explain something. Because this is a real question, Sue answers by giving him information.

🎧 Listen to the excerpts from the news report. Choose the best answer.

Excerpt One

What does Sue's question mean?

a. Do you really believe that Diana counts to 1,000 in four languages and sings songs 1,000 times?

b. It's very difficult to count to 1,000 in four languages and sing songs 1,000 times!! It's unbelievable that Diana can do this!

Excerpt Two

What does Sue's question mean?

a. No one swims in the ocean without a shark cage because it's too dangerous!

b. Do any other swimmers swim in the ocean without a shark cage?

Excerpt Three

What does Jim's question mean?

a. How many people are as determined to reach their goal as Diana Nyad is?

b. Diana Nyad is an extremely determined person! There aren't many people like her!

EXPRESS OPINIONS

Work in small groups. Discuss each question. Be prepared to share your ideas with the class.

1. Why is Diana Nyad so determined to swim from Cuba to Florida? Is it always good to be so determined to reach a goal? Explain your opinion.

2. Why does Diana swim in the ocean without a shark cage?

3. Is Diana a good example for older people?

GO TO MyEnglishLab TO GIVE YOUR OPINION ABOUT ANOTHER QUESTION.

LISTENING TWO AN OUTWARD BOUND EXPERIENCE

COMPREHENSION

Jeremy Manzi is a teenager from New Jersey. He is spending three weeks in the mountains of Wyoming with a group called Outward Bound. In Outward Bound, teenagers learn how to live in nature without beds, TVs, computers, and cell phones. They also learn how to do exciting things outdoors.

Listen to the interview with Jeremy. Complete each sentence. **Two** answers are correct. After you finish, take turns reading the two correct sentences aloud with a partner.

1. Jeremy joined Outward Bound _____.

   a. to meet new people

   b. to experience new things

   c. to prove that he's not a "baby"

2. Jeremy wants to prove to _____ that he can do hard things.

   a. himself

   b. his family

   c. his group leaders

3. Jeremy thinks Outward Bound is great because _____.

    a. he's doing a lot of hard things

    b. the kids help each other and have fun

    c. he walks in the mountains every day

4. Before he went rock climbing, Jeremy _____.

    a. was afraid to do it

    b. was sure that he could do it

    c. thought it was impossible to do it

5. After he went rock climbing, Jeremy _____.

    a. felt that it was really dangerous

    b. felt excited that he did it

    c. felt more confident

6. Jeremy discovered that _____.

    a. he is a strong person

    b. it's exciting to take risks

    c. it's dangerous to take risks

VOCABULARY

Work with a partner. Read the dialog and fill in the blanks with one of the words or phrases from the box. Then practice reading the conversation aloud.

careful	discover	prove (something)	strong	take a risk

A: Why do people like to do dangerous sports like rock climbing and racecar driving?

B: I think those people enjoy doing dangerous things. They think it's very exciting to

_____ .
　　　　1.

A: Yeah, but I think some people want to show the world that they can do something

very dangerous and be successful.

B: Maybe you're right. A lot of risk-takers are trying to _____ to other
　　　　　　　　　　　　　　　　　　　　　　　　　　　　　2.

people. They want to be the first person in the world to do something dangerous.

A: Yeah, like the guy who walked across Niagara Falls on a tightrope.[2] He comes from

a famous family of tightrope walkers. So they always try to _discover_____
　　　　　　　　　　　　　　　　　　　　　　　　　　　　　　　　　　　　3.

new ways to show people the dangerous things they can do.

B: Well, that's their job, right? But I think some people want to do dangerous things

because they're really afraid, and they want to stop feeling that way. After they do

something dangerous, they feel _____ .
　　　　　　　　　　　　　　　　　　4.

A: That's OK if they're successful. But what if they're not _____ and they
　　　　　　　　　　　　　　　　　　　　　　　　　　　　　　　5.

make a mistake? They can really get hurt, or even die! I think it's a little crazy.

B: I know. I'm not interested in doing dangerous things at all!

_____

[2] **tightrope:** a tightly stretched rope or wire high above the ground that a performer walks on

■■■■■■■■■■■■■■■■■■■■■■■■■■ GO TO MyEnglishLab FOR MORE VOCABULARY PRACTICE.

LISTENING SKILL

LISTENING FOR SURPRISING OR UNEXPECTED RESULTS

The conjunction **but** can signal a *contrast* between a cause and a result.

Living in the mountains is difficult, **but** Jeremy isn't having any problems.
[cause]   [result]

However, when we want to make it clear that the *result* is surprising or unexpected, we often use **even though** before **the cause**.

Even though living in the mountains is very difficult, Jeremy is having a great time.
      [cause]   [unexpected result]

OR

Jeremy is having a great time **even though** living in the mountains is very difficult.
[unexpected result]   [cause]

Listen to the example.

Example

Which information is the surprising result?

     a. you can do a lot of things

     b. you're afraid

The correct answer is: **a.** you can do a lot of things.

Explanation

In this sentence, "you're afraid" is the cause, and "you can do a lot of things" is the unexpected or surprising result. This result is unexpected because when people are afraid to do something, they often can't do it. **Even though** makes it clear that this result is not usual or expected.

Listen to the excerpts from the interview. Choose the answer that tells the surprising or unexpected result.

Excerpt One

Which information is the surprising result?

     a. I'm fourteen

     b. everyone thinks I'm the "baby"

(continued on next page)

Excerpt Two

Which information is the surprising result?

    a. it's hard

    b. we're really having a good time

Excerpt Three

Which information is the surprising result?

    a. we're doing difficult things

    b. it's really not dangerous

GO TO MyEnglishLab *FOR MORE SKILL PRACTICE.*

CONNECT THE LISTENINGS

STEP 1: Organize

Diana Nyad, the long-distance swimmer, and Jeremy Manzi, the teenager in Outward Bound, both took risks. How else are they similar? How are they different? Use the information from Listening One and Listening Two to complete the information in the chart.

	DIANA NYAD	JEREMY MANZI
1. How old is she/he?	64	14
2. What risk did she/he take?	long-distance swimming in the ocean without _____ _____	whitewater rafting and _____ _____
3. What was her/his goal?	to be the first person to _____	to have _____ and to learn _____
4. What is she/he trying to prove?	64 is not too old to _____ _____	He's not _____
5. How dangerous was the risk?	0 5 10 not at all so-so very	0 5 10 not at all so-so very
6. How afraid was she/he during the experience?	0 5 10 not at all so-so very	0 5 10 not at all so-so very

STEP 2: Synthesize

Two teenagers on Outward Bound are talking about Diana Nyad's swim to Florida. Use the information in Step One: Organize to continue their conversation. Begin like this:

TEEN 1: Did you hear about Diana Nyad?

TEEN 2: Yeah, I think she's amazing. I can't believe that she's 64 years old!

TEEN 1: You know, even though we're teenagers, we're similar to her in some ways.

TEEN 2: Similar to Diana Nyad? What do you mean?

TEEN 1: Well, she likes to do things that are dangerous. She swam in the ocean without a shark cage. And we're doing some dangerous things, too.

TEEN 2: I don't think rock climbing with Outward Bound is so dangerous. We're very careful and our leaders help us.

TEEN 1: Well, Diana Nyad said that she loves having new challenges.

TEEN 2: OK , we . . . .
But she isn't afraid of anything, and . . .

■■■■■■■■■■■■■■■■■■■■■■■■■■■■■■■■■■■■ *GO TO* MyEnglishLab *TO CHECK WHAT YOU LEARNED.*

3 FOCUS ON SPEAKING

VOCABULARY

REVIEW

Read the homepage of the Adaptive Adventures website on the next page. Complete the text with the words and phrases in the box. Then take turns reading the text aloud with a partner.

careful	determined	strong
challenges	discovered	take a risk
dangerous	proved	unfortunately
decided	reach her goals	

(continued on next page)

Adaptive Adventures—
Adventure programs for children and adults with disabilities

Many people with physical disabilities[3] think that they cannot do any sports. However, at Adaptive Adventures, we believe that *everyone* can do sports! We teach disabled people white water rafting, skiing, snowboarding, and many other exciting outdoor sports. Many disabled people don't do any sports because they think it's too _____ for them; they
1.
are afraid that they will get hurt. However, for the past 12 years, we have

_____ to our students again and again that this is not
2.
true. Our excellent instructors are very _____ when they
3.
teach disabled people, so our students are always safe. In fact, many of our instructors have disabilities, too, so they really understand how their students feel. They also know that many people with disabilities need

new _____ in their lives. When people with disabilities
4.
_____ by trying something new, and they are successful,
5.
it is an exciting experience for them! Many students tell us that after they learned how to do a new sport, they _____ that they felt
6.
much more self-confident—not only about doing sports, but about all parts of their life. Here is what the father of one of our students said about us:

My wife and I both love to ski, so when our daughter was born with a disability, we thought that, _____, she could never enjoy the
7.
sport that we love so much. When she was six, we heard about Adaptive

---

[3] **physical disabilities:** problems with one's body

Adventures, and we ___unfortunately___ to take her to your ski school
8.

for one week. This was the best decision we ever made! We learned that

when your child has a disability, you have to keep teaching her to do new,

more difficult things. This teaches her how to ___reach___. Being
9.

successful helps her to become a ___strong___ and happy person.
10.

Now our daughter says that skiing is easy, and she is ___determined___ to
11.

learn how to snowboard! Thank you Adaptive Adventures!

EXPAND

Adjectives that end in -**ed** usually describe people's feelings. Adjectives that end in -**ing** usually describe people, things, or situations.

I was **amazed** when I heard about Diana Nyad. She is an **amazing** swimmer.

Here are some common -**ed** and -**ing** adjectives:

amazed	challenging	excited	interested	surprising
amazing	determined	exciting	interesting	tired
bored	disappointed	frightened	scared	tiring
boring	disappointing	frightening	surprised	worried

Complete the sentences using any of the adjectives from the list. More than one answer may be possible. Be sure to use the correct form. Compare your answers with a partner's.

1. Diana Nyad thinks that long-distance swimming is _boring / challenging / tiring_.

2. In my opinion, long-distance swimming is very ___challenging___.

3. Jeremy thought that rock climbing was ___exciting___.

4. After he climbed up the mountain, Jeremy felt ___determined___.

5. If my son or daughter goes rock climbing, I will feel ___worried___.

(continued on next page)

6. Doing new things for the first time can be ___amazing___.

7. Doing the same thing again and again is ___boring___.

8. People who never stop trying to reach their goal are very ___disappointed___

9. People were very ___surprised___ in hearing Diana Nyad's story.

10. When Diana couldn't finish her swim the fourth time, she probably felt very ___disappointed___.

CREATE

Work in small groups. Ask and answer the questions. Use the vocabulary from Review and Expand.

1. Did you ever **take a risk**? What kind of **risk** was it? (Risks are not always physical. They can be mental, financial, cultural, or involve relationships with other people.) Were you successful? How did you feel?

2. Did you ever do anything **dangerous**? What was it? Were you **careful**? How did you feel?

3. Did you ever feel very **determined** to do something? What was it? Were you successful? How did you feel?

4. Did you ever **discover** something about yourself? What was it? How did you **discover** it?

■■■■■■■■■■■■■■■■■■■■■■■■■■■■■■■ *GO TO* MyEnglishLab *FOR MORE VOCABULARY PRACTICE.*

GRAMMAR

1 Read the excerpts from the radio news report. Follow the directions.

a. We're speaking to you from a boat.

b. She is still swimming even though things are not going very well right now.

c. Diana's wearing a special wetsuit.

d. I'm doing a lot of really hard things.

e. You're discovering some new things about yourself.

1. Underline the verbs in sentences a–e.

2. What are the two parts of the verb? _____ + _____

3. What form of *be* is used after each subject?

I _____   We _____

You _____   They _____

He/She/It _____   Things _____

Diana _____

4. Which sentences from question 1 tell about an action right now/at this moment? Which sentences tell about a change that is happening these days (but not at this moment)?

PRESENT CONTINUOUS

1. Use the present continuous tense to describe actions or situations that are happening:	
a. right now, at this moment, or	**a.** She **is** still **swimming** even though things **are not going** very well.
b. now, as in this week, this month, this semester, this year, or these days.	**b.** You**'re discovering** some new things about yourself.
2. To form the present continuous, use the **present tense of the *be* verb + the -*ing* form of the main verb**.	I**'m doing** a lot of really hard things.
a. If the **main verb ends in -*e***, like *have*, drop the -*e* and add -*ing*.	**Is** she **having** problems breathing?
b. The verb *swim* has a consonant/vowel/consonant pattern at the end. Double the final consonant before -*ing*. Similar verbs include *get, begin, put, run,* and *stop*.	Diana Nyad **is swimming** from Cuba to Florida.
3. For negative sentences, use the ***be* verb + *not*** (or *n't*) + **the main verb**.	She **is not giving** up. Things **aren't going** very well.

(continued on next page)

4. For *yes/no* questions, put the *be* verb before the subject.

Is she **swimming?**

You can answer *yes/no* questions with a **short** answer: **subject + *be* verb.**

Yes, **she is.**

5. For *wh-* questions, use the **question word + *be* verb + subject + main verb.**

Where is she **swimming?**
What are you **doing?**

6. Stative (non-action) verbs are **not** used in present continuous, even though the action is happening right now.

    a. Some common verbs that are **always** stative (non-action) are: *be, believe, hate, know, like, love, mean, need, understand,* and *want.*

Diana **knows** how to clear her mind.
She **likes** challenges!

    b. Some verbs have two meanings: a *non-action* meaning and an *action* meaning. Some common verbs with both meanings are: *feel, have, look, see, smell, taste,* and *think.*

Everyone **thinks** I'm the "baby."
Diana is counting. She **isn't thinking** about anything.

    c. When the verb *have* is used in some expressions, it has an **action meaning**, and it **can** be used in present continuous.

She **is having difficulty** breathing.
We**'re having** a good time.

    Some common expressions are: *have trouble, have difficulty, have problems, have fun, have a good time* and *have a party.*

---

2 Work with a partner. Fill in the blanks with the correct form of the verb in parentheses. Use present continuous for action verbs, and simple present for non-action verbs. Then read the dialog aloud.

A: Hi. What _____?
                 1. (you / do)

B: I _____ Diana Nyad, the famous swimmer.
         2. (watch)

A: _____ from Cuba to Florida again?
    3. (she / swim)

B: Yes! This is her fifth time, and this time she's finally going to make it. She

_____ the last few feet right now. This _____
       4. (swim)   5. (be)
so exciting!

A: Look, she _____ up and _____ out of the
                 6. (stand)   7. (get)
water. She did it!

B: I _____. I can't believe it. And look at all the people on the
       8. (know)
beach. They _____ and _____.
            9. (cheer)   10. (scream)

A: But look at Diana's face. Wow, she _____ terrible. She's
                                          11. (look)
really sunburned and she _____ standing up. Her friend
                          12. (have trouble)
_____ her to walk.
13. (help)

B: Well, that's because she's so tired. She just swam for 53 hours!

A: But she _____ now. It looks like she _____ to
              14. (smile)   15. (want)
say something. A reporter _____ over to talk to her.
                           16. (go)

REPORTER 1:   Sixty-four-year-old Diana Nyad has just finished her historic swim from

Havana, Cuba, to Key West, Florida. She is the first person in the world to

do this without a shark cage, and she is also the first person in the world to

swim for 53 hours!

REPORTER 2:   Diana, congratulations! Millions of people all over the world

_____ you on TV right now and they
        17. (watch)

_____ all so excited that you reached your goal!
        18. (be)

Do _____ something to say to all the people who
     19. (you / have)

_____ you and _____ you right now?
        20. (love)   21. (watch)

DIANA: I've got three messages. One is "we should never, ever give up." Two is "you

_____ never too old to chase your dreams." And three is
        22. (be)

"it _____ like a solitary⁴ sport, but it's a team [effort]."
     23. (look)

---

⁴ **solitary:** for only one person

■■■■■■■■■■■■■■■■■■■■■■■■■■■■■■■■■■■*GO TO* MyEnglishLab *FOR MORE GRAMMAR PRACTICE.*

PRONUNCIATION

THE VOWEL SOUNDS /iy/ AND /ɪ/ (*EATS* AND *IT'S*)

To pronounce /iy/, the front of your tongue is very high in your mouth. Your lips are spread and tense, like a smile.

To pronounce /ɪ/, the front of your tongue is slightly (a little bit) lower. Your lips are relaxed.

1 ⊙ Listen and repeat these words with the sound /iy/.

be, we, she, see, *eat, even, easy*

keep, mean, meet, teach, reach, dream

here, clear, years

we'll, feel, deal

*people, really, lead*er, *breathing*

agree, be*lieve*

2 ⊙ Listen and repeat these words with the sound /ɪ/.

if, in, is, it, it's

did, big, give, wind, with, this, sick, fish, swim, think, things

will, still

*did*n't, *giving, dis*tance, *dif*ferent, *mid*dle

*finishes, diffi*cult

con*ditions,* con*tinue*

3 ⊙ Listen and repeat these pairs of words with /iy/ and /ɪ/.

	A	B		A	B
1.	eat	it	**6.**	we'll	will
2.	eats	it's	**7.**	feel	fill
3.	ease	is	**8.**	deed	did
4.	reach	rich	**9.**	seek	sick
5.	leave	live	**10.**	these	this

4 Take turns with a partner. Read one of the words from each pair in Exercise 3. Your partner will tell you if you pronounced the word from Column A (/iy/) or Column B (/ɪ/).

5 Work with a partner. Student A, read the beginning of each sentence in Column A. Student B, don't look at Column A. Listen to Student A and choose the best ending in Column B. Change roles after number 6. Notice the syllables with /iy/ and /ɪ/. Be careful to pronounce them clearly.

A	**B**
1. *Did* Diana *swim* to Florida com*pletely* alone?	some*thing* to *eat*.
2. There were thirty *people* . . .	because man*y* jel*lyfish bit* her.
3. Ever*y* hour, the *team* gave Diana . . .	on Diana's *team*.
4. One person on the *team* used a special ma*chine* . . .	unfortunate*ly*, *it didn*'t cover her *lips*.
5. Diana had trouble *swimming* . . .	No, *she* had a *team* on a boat.
6. *Even* though Diana wore a special wetsuit over her bo*dy*, . . .	to *keep* the sharks away from Diana.

Switch roles. | Switch roles.

7. When the jel*lyfish bit* Diana on her *lips*, . . .	Diana *didn*'t want to *give* up.
8. Diana con*tinued swimming*, . . .	Diana *did* not *leave* the water once.
9. *Even* though *she* felt tired and *sick*, . . .	*it* made her *feel* very *sick*.
10. For *fifty-three* hours,	"You're help*ing me* to *reach* new goals."
11. Just before Diana *reached Key* West, . . .	even though *she* had trouble *breathing*.
12. Man*y* men and *women* write to Diana to say, . . .	*she* stopped *swimming* for a few *minutes* and said thank you to her *team*.

SPEAKING SKILL

EXPRESSING UNEXPECTED RESULTS WITH *EVEN THOUGH*

To show that a result is unusual or not expected, we often use the words **even though** before the cause.

Example

Even though things are not going very well, Diana is still swimming.
                [cause]   [result]

OR

Diana is still swimming **even though** things are not going very well.
    [result]   [cause]

Remember: Do not use the word *but* when you use *even though*.

Even though things are not going very well, ~~but~~ Diana is still swimming.

1 Take turns with a partner. Choose the correct result for each cause. Remember, when you use **even though**, the result must be surprising or unexpected. Read the sentences aloud.

1. Even though I'm a very good swimmer, _____.

   a. I'm afraid to swim in the ocean

   b. I like to swim in the ocean

2. Even though I tried very hard, _____.

   a. I reached my goal

   b. I didn't reach my goal

3. _____ even though it's dangerous.

   a. I like to go rock climbing

   b. I don't like to go rock climbing

4. _____ even though I was frightened.

   a. I'm happy that I went whitewater rafting

   b. I'm happy that I didn't go whitewater rafting

2 Work with a partner. Read these sentences about Diana Nyad. Then connect the sentences using **even though**. Decide which sentence tells the cause and which sentence tells the result. Remember to put **even though** before the cause. Read the sentences aloud.

Example

Diana was very tired. She continued to swim.
       [cause]   [result]

Even though *Diana was very tired, she continued to swim.*
OR
*Diana continued to swim **even though** she was very tired.*

1. Diana is an amazing swimmer. She is 64 years old.

2. Diana tried four times and was not successful. She wanted to try again.

3. Diana swam for more than 50 hours. It was very difficult.

4. There were dangerous sharks in the ocean. Diana swam without a shark cage.

5. The jellyfish bit Diana. She wore a special wetsuit.

6. The swim from Cuba was long and difficult. Diana was so happy that she did it.

3 Complete each sentence with a cause or an unexpected result that makes sense. Then, compare your sentences with a partner.

1. Even though I'm afraid of high places, I _____.

2. I want to join Outward Bound even though _____.

3. Some people enjoy taking risks even though _____.

4. I decided to _____ even though _____.

5. Even though _____, I'm very determined to do it.

6. Some people are afraid to fly in airplanes even though _____.

■■■■■■■■■■■■■■■GO TO MyEnglishLab *FOR MORE SKILL PRACTICE AND TO CHECK WHAT YOU LEARNED.*

FINAL SPEAKING TASK

A role play is a short performance. The students take on roles, or become characters, and act out a situation.

In this activity, you are going to role-play an interview with a risk-taker.

Use the vocabulary, grammar, pronunciation, and language for expressing unexpected results from this unit.*

You are going to role-play an interview between a TV news reporter and a risk-taker.

STEP 1: Together with the class, think of at least six interesting questions to ask the risk-taker. Write them down.

STEP 2: Work with a partner. Student A, you are a TV news reporter. You are interviewing a risk-taker **while she/he is doing something very challenging or dangerous.** Use the questions that you wrote down in Step 1 and any others you want to ask.

Student B, you are a risk-taker. You can be an athlete, an entertainer, or any other person who is doing something very challenging or dangerous. You can also be yourself if you can tell about a time that you took a risk. (Remember that a risk or challenge is not always physical.) Answer the questions that the TV news reporter asks you.

---

* For Alternative Speaking Topics, see page 161.

STEP 3: When you are finished, change roles. Student A, choose a different risk-taker to role-play. Student B, you are the TV news reporter.

■ ■ ■ ■ ■ ■ ■ ■ ■ ■ ■ ■ ■ *GO TO* MyEnglishLab *FOR MORE SKILL PRACTICE AND TO CHECK WHAT YOU LEARNED.*

UNIT PROJECT

Choose one of the people on the list to research. Find three or four photos of the person doing something challenging or dangerous. Then report to the class or a small group.

Christiane Amanpour	Philippe Petit
Felix Baumgartner	Jordan Romero
Sarah Burke	Nick Vujicic
James Cameron	Stephen Wampler
Yuichiro Miura	Malala Yousafazi
Danica Patrick	

STEP 1: Give some background information.

Who is this person? Where is she/he from? How old is she/he? What did she/he do? (What was her/his goal?) Why did she/he do it? Did she/he set a new record? What are her/his future plans? Why did she/he want to take a risk?

- to feel a challenge?
- to entertain people?
- to continue a family tradition?

- to set a new record?
- to become famous?
- to prove something? (what?)

STEP 2: Tell about the photos.

Show three or four photos of the risk-taker while she/he is doing something challenging. Try to find photos that show the person at different points (beginning, middle, and end). Explain exactly what the person is doing in each photo.

Use these expressions to begin some of your sentences:

- Please look at (this / the first / the second / the third) photo. In this photo, X is . . .

- As you can see, X is . . .

- If you look at (this / the first / the second / the third) photo, you can see that X is . . .

Step 1: I'm going to tell you about Nik Wallenda. He is American, and he is the seventh generation in his family of tightrope walkers. The Wallenda family is famous for doing very dangerous things. Nik Wallenda is an entertainer, and he is continuing his family tradition. He always tries to set new records.

Step 2: Please look at the first photo. **In this photo**, Nik Wallenda is beginning to walk across Niagara Falls. He is walking on a tightrope. **As you can see**, he is wearing everyday clothes. He is holding a very long stick. It helps him to keep his balance.

Photo 1

If you look at the second photo, you can see that Wallenda is standing in the middle of the tightrope. Even though he is doing something very dangerous, he is smiling and he looks very calm. Even though it is very windy, he is still putting one foot in front of the other.

Photo 2

(continued on next page)

Now, please look at the third photo. Wallenda is close to the end of the walk. **As you can see in this photo**, he is kneeling down on the tightrope. He is thanking God for helping him to reach his goal. Wallenda always does this at the end of each walk. Even though he is a professional, I think it's still very dangerous to walk over Niagara Falls on a tightrope. I think Wallenda is amazing!

Photo 3

Listening Task

Listen to your classmates' presentations. Ask questions. Try to use some of the new language from this unit.

ALTERNATIVE SPEAKING TOPICS

Discuss one of the topics. Use the grammar, vocabulary, pronunciation, and language for expressing unexpected results from this unit.

1. "Please know that I am aware of the hazards.[5] I want to do it because I want to do it. Women must try to do things as men have tried. When they fail, their failure must be a challenge to others."—Amelia Earhart, American (1897–1937)

   Explain this quote by Amelia Earhart. What does she mean? Do you agree with her? Why or why not?

2. Did you ever do any dangerous sports? Did you ever live in nature, without a cell phone, computer, TV, etc.? Tell about your experiences. If you never did these things, do you want to? Why or why not?

3. There are many famous sayings and quotes about determination and challenges. Look at the list below. Explain what each saying or quote means and give an example. Then tell if you agree or disagree with it, and explain why.

   a. If at first you don't succeed, try, try again.

   b. Where there's a will,[6] there's a way.

   c. I've failed over and over and over again in my life and that is why I succeed. —Michael Jordan

   d. I hated every minute of training, but I said, "Don't quit. Suffer[7] now and live the rest of your life as a champion."—Muhammad Ali

   e. Take risks: if you win, you will be happy; if you lose, you will be wise.[8]

---

[5] **hazards:** dangers
[6] **Where there's a will:** When you feel determined
[7] **suffer:** feel pain, feel very bad
[8] **wise:** intelligent; smart

■ ■ ■ ■ ■ ■ ■ ■ ■ ■ ■ GO TO MyEnglishLab TO DISCUSS ONE OF THE ALTERNATIVE TOPICS, WATCH A VIDEO ABOUT A HEROIC PILOT, AND TAKE THE UNIT 6 ACHIEVEMENT TEST. ■ ■ ■ ■ ■ ■ ■ ■ ■ ■ ■ ■ ■ ■ ■ ■ ■ ■

ONLY CHILD—
Lonely Child?

1 FOCUS ON THE TOPIC

1. Read the title of the unit. What is an *only child*? What does the title mean?

2. In your country, how many children do *most* families have?

3. How many students in the class are only children? How many students have one brother or sister? Two? Three or more?

■■■■■■■■■■■■■■■■■■■■■■■■■■■■■■■■■ GO TO MyEnglishLab TO CHECK WHAT YOU KNOW.

VOCABULARY

1 Lisa and Jules Conner are the parents of an only child. They started a new blog for one-child families. Work with a partner. Read the conversation that they posted on their blog. Choose the correct word for each blank.

A Conversation with the Bloggers: *Lisa and Jules Conner*

HOME

CONTACT

ABOUT US

Lisa: Welcome to "Our Only Child!" "Our Only Child" is the first blog for families like us—happy families with just one child. We started this blog because we want to share information with other one-child families.

Lisa, Jules, and Jonathan Conner

Jules: Many people think that only children are _____

1. (intelligent / lonely)

because they don't have _____. However, we all know

2. (a baby / siblings)

that this is not true!

Lisa: Of course it's not true! We can spend a lot of time with our children

because we don't have to _____ other children. Many

3. (afford / take care of)

parents with large families don't have enough time to do this, especially if both

parents work full-time. Parents with one child don't have this problem.

Jules: We also know that friends are very important to only children. Many of us move to neighborhoods with lots of young families, so our children can make a lot of friends.

Lisa: We also want to share information from the latest studies about one-child families. Here's some very interesting information: Only 3 percent of the American _____ say that a one-child family is
                   4. (population / personal)
the best family size. But recently, *Time Magazine* said that one-third (33 percent) of young Americans plan to _____ just one
                                 5. (have / make)
_____ after they _____ .
   6. (child / money)   7. (get married / take care of)

Jules: Why is this? Of course, every family is different, so this is a very
_____ decision for every couple. But life in most
  8. (personal / population)
American cities today is expensive. It costs between $286,000 and $324,000 to
_____ a child to age 18 in the U.S.—and that's before
     9. (raise / have)
paying for college! Many parents today don't _____
                                  10. (have / make)
enough _____ at their jobs, so they
     11. (children / money)
_____ to have a big family.
12. (can't afford / make money)

Lisa: That's one reason that many Americans today are
_____ the _____ decision to have
  13. (having / making)   14. (time / responsible)
just one child and to give their child the best life possible!

Lisa Conner   Jules Conner
Bloggers, *Our Only Child*

2 🎧 Now listen to the conversation and check your answers. Then read the conversation aloud with a partner.

3 Match the vocabulary on the left with the correct definition on the right. Write the letter of the correct definition on the line.

_____ 1. can't afford

_____ 2. get married

_____ 3. have a child

_____ 4. lonely

_____ 5. make a decision

_____ 6. make money

_____ 7. personal

_____ 8. population

_____ 9. raise

_____ 10. responsible

_____ 11. sibling

_____ 12. take care of

a. brother or sister

b. decide; choose

c. do everything that someone needs; watch over

d. have a husband or wife; marry (someone)

e. right or correct for a certain situation

f. bring up a child; give a child a home, food, clothing, and education until the age of 18

g. don't have enough money (to do something)

h. give birth to a baby

i. individual; different for every person

j. sad because you are alone

k. earn money from your job

l. the number of people in a city, country, the world

GO TO MyEnglishLab *FOR MORE VOCABULARY PRACTICE.*

PREVIEW

Listen to the beginning of *Changing Families*, a TV talk show. Then answer the questions. The host, Maria Sanchez, is going to talk to two families.

1. Maria is probably going to ask the parents, "Why did you decide to ____?"

    a. have children

    b. have only one child

2. What are Maria and the families going to talk about? Check (✓) your ideas.

____ siblings	____ teachers
____ culture	____ grandparents
____ decisions	____ travel
____ money	____ friends
____ age	____ feelings

MAIN IDEAS

1 🎧 Listen to the complete interview. Now look at your answers in Preview on page 167. Were any of your answers correct? Did they help you to understand the interview?

2 🎧 Listen to the interview again. Complete the sentences with the words and phrases from the box. You will not use all of the words and phrases.

a good life	a lot of money	difficult	lonely
a happy child	busy	easy	siblings

1. Today, many people don't believe that only children are _____lonely_____.

2. For Marion and Mark, raising a young child is ____difficult____.

3. Marion and Mark think Tonia is __a happy child__.

4. Tom and Jenna can afford to give one child __a good life__.

5. Jay is usually _____busy_____ with his friends, sports, and music.

DETAILS

Listen again. Write **T** (true) or **F** (false). Correct the false information.

_____ 1. There are more only children in big cities.

_____ 2. Marion had a baby when she was 36.

_____ 3. Marion and Mark can't take care of Tonia.

_____ 4. Tonia spends time with her parents and friends.

_____ 5. Tonia is a very popular child.

_____ 6. Maria read that only children are more interesting than children with siblings.

_____ 7. In 2050, there are going to be 90 million people in the world.

_____ 8. Jenna and Tom made a difficult decision.

_____ 9. School, music, and traveling are important to Jenna and Tom.

_____ 10. Sometimes Jay is lonely.

■■■■■■■■■■■■■■■■■■■■■■■■■■■■■■■■■**GO TO** MyEnglishLab **FOR MORE LISTENING PRACTICE.**

MAKE INFERENCES

MAKING INFERENCES BASED ON WORD CHOICES

An inference is a guess about something that is not directly stated. To make an inference, use information that you understand from what you hear.

We can usually understand what people mean or how they feel even if they don't explain everything directly. Their *word choices* often help us to *infer* their meaning or feeling.

Listen to the example.

Example

1. What can we infer/understand about Mark?

   a. After Tonia was born, he and Marion thought about having another child.

   b. After Tonia was born, he and Marion never thought about having another child.

(continued on next page)

Only Child—Lonely Child? 169

2. Which word(s) helped you to understand this? _____

The correct answers are: 1. **a**, 2. decided

Explanation

Mark said, "**At some point, we just decided** that we couldn't take care of Tonia *and* a new baby." The word *decided* helps us to understand that he and Marion **thought about and discussed** having another baby (but then they decided not to have one).

🎧 Listen to the excerpts from the TV talk show. Circle the correct answer to complete each sentence.

Excerpt One

    1. What can we infer about Marion and Mark?

        a. They feel too old to raise a second child.

        b. They want to raise another young child.

    2. Which word(s) helped you to understand this? _____

Excerpt Two

    1. What does Maria want people to understand?

        a. There is new information about only children that many people don't know.

        b. People already know everything about only children.

    2. Which word(s) helped you to understand this? _____

Excerpt Three

    1. What does Jenna want to explain?

        a. Money is more important to them now than in the past.

        b. Their son needs a lot of expensive things.

    2. Which word(s) helped you to understand this? _____

EXPRESS OPINIONS

Read the statements. Mark each one **A** (Agree) or **D** (Disagree). Then discuss your opinions with the class.

_____ **1.** It's better for children to have young parents.

_____ **2.** Only children are more popular than children with siblings.

_____ **3.** People need to think about the population problem in the world when they decide how many children to have.

GO TO MyEnglishLab TO GIVE YOUR OPINION ABOUT ANOTHER QUESTION.

LISTENING TWO   HOW DO ONLY KIDS FEEL?

COMPREHENSION

Now listen to Tonia and Jay, two only children. They are speaking to Maria Sanchez. Circle the best answer to complete each sentence.

Tonia

1. Tonia _____ being an only child.

    a. likes

    b. loves

    c. doesn't like

2. Most of Tonia's friends have _____.

    a. siblings

    b. sisters

    c. older parents

3. Tonia's mother _____ her decision to Tonia.

    a. didn't explain

    b. explained

    c. isn't going to explain

(continued on next page)

4. How does Tonia feel about her parents' decision? She _____.

   a. understands it and agrees with it

   b. understands it but isn't happy about it

   c. doesn't understand it

5. Jay and Tonia have _____ feelings about being only children.

   a. unusual

   b. the same

   c. different

6. When Jay spends time with his parents, he feels _____.

   a. different

   b. special

   c. uncomfortable

Jay

7. Jay and his parents enjoy _____.

   a. traveling

   b. living in Asia

   c. staying home

8. Many of Jay's friends don't like to _____.

   a. do things alone

   b. spend time with their parents

   c. cry like a baby

VOCABULARY

Take turns with a partner. Student A, read your sentence. Student B, use one of the words in the box to help you to respond to Student A in a complete sentence. You will also need to add your own words.

act	alone	have fun	mature	opportunities

1. **A:** Why did Jay's family decide to move to Chicago?

   B: They wanted Jay to take classes in music and art, but their small town didn't
   _____.

2. **A:** Lisa is only 11, but she reads the newspaper every day, and she can discuss the
   news like an adult.

   B: I know. She _____. Most 11-year-old kids aren't interested in the
   news at all.

3. **A:** I'm worried about Ryan. His teacher said he was mean to one of his classmates
   today.

   B: Really? How did _____?

4. **A:** There is an international party at my school tonight. Do you want to come?

   B: Yes, thanks! That sounds great. I'm sure _____.

5. **A:** I'm really sorry that I can't go to the soccer match with you tomorrow.

   B: Please don't worry about it. I can _____. It's not a problem for me.

■■■■■■■■■■■■■■■■■■■■■■■■■■■ GO TO MyEnglishLab FOR MORE VOCABULARY PRACTICE.

LISTENING SKILL

USING GRAPHIC ORGANIZERS

When you listen to a lecture, it's a good idea to take notes so you can remember the information. A chart, or a graphic organizer, can help you to organize the information you hear.

You know that Maria is going to ask Tonia and Jay questions, so it's useful to make a chart like the one on page 174 to write their answers.

Questions for Only Children	Tonia	Jay
1. Age?	8	12
2. Feelings about being an only child?	She _____.	

🎧 Listen to the beginning of the excerpt. What is Tonia's answer to question 2? Write her answer under her name in the chart.

Example

The correct answer is: **She hates it.**

🎧 Listen to the rest of the interview. In the chart, write four questions that Maria asks. Then fill in Tonia's and Jay's answers. Compare your chart with a partner's. What did your partner write in the chart? When you finish, compare all the charts with the class.

Questions for Only Children	Tonia	Jay
1. Age?	8	12
2. Feelings about being an only child?	She hates it.	He _____.
3.		
4.		
5.		
6.		

▪▪▪▪▪▪▪▪▪▪▪▪▪▪▪▪▪▪▪▪▪▪▪▪▪▪▪▪▪ *GO TO* MyEnglishLab *FOR MORE SKILL PRACTICE.*

STEP 1: Organize

What are the advantages of having only one child? What are the advantages of being an only child? Think about Listening One and Listening Two. Write the advantages in the chart or on a sheet of paper. Use the cues in each box to make a complete sentence. Then compare your chart with a partner's. Number 1 has been done for you.

ADVANTAGES FOR PARENTS	ADVANTAGES FOR ONLY CHILDREN
1. In big cities, / less expensive / raise / one *In big cities, it's less expensive to raise just one child.*	1. In big cities, only children / have / opportunities *In big cities, only children may have more opportunities.*
2. Parents / afford / give / only children / a good	2. Some only children / special
3. For older parents, / it / easier / raise / just one	3. Only children / learn / enjoy / spend / alone
4. Parents / spend / more time / an / child	4. Only children / more popular and intelligent / children / siblings
5. It / more responsible / have / child because of / population	5. Only children / more mature / children with siblings

STEP 2: Synthesize

Student A thinks it's good to have **more than one** child. Student B thinks it's better to have **only one child**. Role-play. Work with a partner. Complete the conversation orally with information from Step 1: Organize. Add five more lines for Student A and for Student B. Begin like this:

A: Do you really believe that it's best to have just one child?

B: Of course, especially in big cities. It's less expensive to raise just one child in a big city.

A: That's true. In big cities, parents can afford to give their children more . . .

B: Also, parents with only one child can spend . . .

A: Well, that's true. But some children really want a sibling.

B: Yes, but . . .

A: . . .

GO TO MyEnglishLab TO CHECK WHAT YOU LEARNED.

VOCABULARY

REVIEW

Work in pairs. Student A, read your sentence aloud. Student B, read your sentence aloud and fill in the blank with the correct word from the box.

decision	lonely	~~raise~~	tired
had fun	personal	took care of	

A: Did both of your parents work when you were a child?

B: Yes, but my grandmother lived with us. She helped my parents to

_____*raise*_____ me.
     1.

A: Really? That's unusual in the U.S.

B: I know, but my parents are both doctors. They worked a lot, and when they came

home, they were really _____.
               2.

A: Sure . . .

B: So my grandmother _____ me during the week.
            3.

A: Did you like that?

B: Yes, I loved it. She always had a lot of time to play with me, and we always

_____ together. I was never _____.
     4.   5.

A: That's great.

B: Yeah, and we also talked a lot about so many things. My grandmother always

helped me if I had a _____ problem, and she taught me how to make
                6.

the best _____.
       7.

A: You were lucky!

B: Yeah, I agree.

Now switch roles.

can't afford	have	opportunities
got married	make a lot of money	take care of

B: Did I tell you the news about my brother and sister-in-law[1]?

A: No. What's happening with them?

B: Well, you know that they _____ a year ago, right?
                                                 7.

A: Yeah . . .

B: Well, now they're going to _____ a baby!
                                           8.

A: That's great!

B: I know. I can't believe it!

A: It's very exciting. Is Joan going to stop working after she has the baby?

B: I think she's going to stay home for three months and then she's going to go back to

work. They _____ to live on just one salary.
                              9.

A: Really? Doesn't your brother have a good job?

B: Well, he loves his job, and he has a lot of _____ to travel, but
                                                 10.

unfortunately, he doesn't _____!
                                   11.

A: Oh, so I guess they're going to get a babysitter.

B: Yeah, and my mother is going to help them to _____ the baby, too.
                                                12.

A: That's nice.

---

[1] **sister-in law:** your brother's wife or your spouse's sister

1 This is a page from the Conners' blog, "Our Only Child." Read Columns A and B.

A

Some people think that only children have a lot of problems.

They say:

"Problem" #1:

*Only children are **selfish**.*

Only children get all of their parents' attention, so they think they are the most important people in the world. They never think about other people. These children are **selfish**. This means

_____.

"Problem" #2:

*Only children are **spoiled**.*

Parents of only children are sad that their child has no siblings. They think that toys, money, and other things can make their child feel happy. But the child keeps asking for more and more. These children are **spoiled**. This means _____.

"Problem" #3:

*Only children **don't get along well with** other children.*

Only children live with adults, so they don't learn how to act like children. They act like "little adults." They don't learn how to play with other children, and they don't feel comfortable with them. Only children **don't get along well with** other children. This means_____.

B

Parents of only children know this is not true!

We say:

_____ *We and our children are happy with our families. We don't need to buy our children lots of toys to make them happy. But our children spend more time playing by themselves, so they learn how to be alone. They are more **independent** than children with siblings. This means _____.*

*Our children are usually more mature than other children their age, but we know that it's very important for them to have friends. We make sure that our children always have friends to play with. Our children are usually very popular with other children. They **have many close friends**. This means _____.*

_____*We give our children a lot of attention. This makes our children feel good about themselves. They also care about other people. Our children are usually **self-confident**, not selfish. This means ____.*

2 Match the vocabulary **in bold** with the correct definitions below. Write the letter of the correct definition in the blank at the end of each paragraph. Then, check your answers with a partner.

Definitions:

a. they have a lot of very good friends

b. they can do many things without help

c. they think only about themselves

d. they believe they are good people, with good abilities

e. they have problems with other children

f. they are never satisfied. They always want more and more things

3 Work with a partner. Match the problem in Column A with the best response by the "Our Only Child" bloggers in Column B. Write the number of the problem on the line in front of the best response.

4 Change partners. Take turns reading the problems and responses aloud with your new partner. Student A, read one problem. Then Student B, read the correct response. Check with your teacher if you have different responses to the problems.

CREATE

Work with a small group of students. Talk about each idea in the blog post. Which ideas do you think are true? Why? Use the vocabulary from Review and Expand.

Example
Only children are selfish. / Only children are self-confident.

STUDENT A: I think most only children are selfish. It's natural. Only children spend a lot of time alone. They don't learn how to think about other people's feelings. That's why they are selfish.

STUDENT B: I'm not sure about that. In my opinion, . . .

STUDENT C: I . . . because . . .

1. Only children are spoiled. / Only children are independent.

2. Only children don't act like children. / Only children are mature.

3. Only children don't get along well with other children. / Only children have many close friends.

GO TO MyEnglishLab *FOR MORE VOCABULARY PRACTICE.*

GRAMMAR

1 Read Maria's sentences. Look at the underlined verbs. Then answer the questions.

MARIA: Today we're <u>going to talk</u> about only children.

MARIA: Next, I'm <u>going to talk</u> to the kids.

1. How many parts does each verb have?

2. What is the first part?

3. What is the second part? Does it change?

4. What's the form of the last part?

THE FUTURE WITH *BE GOING TO*

1. Use *be + going to* + the base form of the verb to talk about an action in the future.	I **am going to have** lunch later. He **is going to visit** friends tonight.
NOTE: Use contractions in speaking and in informal writing.	**I'm going to have** lunch later. He**'s going to visit** friends tonight.
2. To make a negative sentence, put *not* before *going to*.	I'm **not going to** travel next week. She's **not going to** have a big family.
NOTE: You can also use the negative contractions *isn't* and *aren't*.	He **isn't going to** get married soon. We **aren't going to** have a big family.
3. To make questions, put a form of *be* before the **subject**.	**Are you** going to visit us soon? **Where is he** going to go next year?
4. To answer *yes/no* questions, you can use a short form: *Yes* + subject + *be* *No* + subject + *be* + *not*	Yes, I am / he is / you are / we are / they are. No, I'm not / he's not / you're not / we're not / they're not.
NOTE: You can also use the negative contractions *isn't* and *aren't*.	No, he **isn't**. / No, they **aren't**.
5. You can use these future time expressions with *be going to*: later/ tonight / tomorrow / soon in two days / in a week / in a month / in a year this Tuesday / week / month / year next Monday / week / month / year	**I'm going to** move to a different city **next year**. We**'re going to** have dinner together **this week**.

---

2 Tonia is talking about her plans for the future. Complete the conversation with the correct forms of **be going to**. Then read the conversation aloud with a partner.

MARIA: I know you don't like being an only child. So, _____ you
          1.
          _____ have a big family when you grow up?

TONIA: Yes, definitely! I _____ have four or five kids! Maybe six!
          2.

MARIA: Well, then your children _____ be lonely!
          3.

TONIA: Right. They _____ have a lot of brothers and sisters to play
          4.
          with.

MARIA: But, you know, raising so many kids is very expensive!

TONIA: Well, I _____ work hard and save a lot of money. I
          5.
          _____ be rich!
          6.

MARIA: You _____ be rich? That's amazing!
          7.

3 Work with a small group of students.

1. On a small piece of paper, write a question using **be going to** and a phrase from columns A and B. Put all questions in a paper bag. Give your bag to another group.

2. Take turns. Choose a question from the bag. Read it aloud. The next student has to answer it using **be going to**. Ask and answer all the questions in the bag.

A	**B**
go shopping	this year
take a vacation	next week
move to a different city/country	in a month
move to the countryside	soon
see a movie	tonight
study another language	tomorrow
buy a car	in _____ years
have a big family	this weekend
get a new job	in the future

Examples

Are you going to move to a different city this year?

Are you going to see a movie tonight?

■ ■ ■ ■ ■ ■ GO TO MyEnglishLab FOR MORE GRAMMAR PRACTICE.

PRONUNCIATION

PRONOUNCING *GOING TO*

🎧 Native speakers pronounce *going to* in two ways. Listen to the sentences. How is *going to* pronounced?

A: I'm going to take a vacation next month. (pronounced /gówɪŋtə/)

B: I'm going to see you later! (pronounced /gə́nə/)

- In formal or careful (slow) speech, use the full form: *going to* /gówɪŋtə/

  In today's lecture, I'm going to speak about only children.

- In informal or fast speech, use the reduced (short) form: *gonna* /gə́nə/

  I'm gonna ask my mom if you can come for dinner.

NOTE: 1. We do not write *gonna* in formal (academic or business) English. *Gonna* is written only in very informal writing, such as text messages (SMS).

2. Pronounce *gonna* only when it means "future," and there is another verb. When *going* is the only verb in the sentence, you cannot use the reduced form.

   Example

   a. I'm ***going to*** see you later! ("gonna" is OK here.)

   b. I'm ***going to*** class now. ("gonna" is impossible here. You must pronounce it /gówɪŋtə/.)

3. You can use /gówɪŋtə/ (the careful pronunciation) when you speak if it's more comfortable for you.

1 🎧 Listen to the sentences. Is **going to** pronounced in the full form or the reduced form (**gonna**)? Circle the correct answer. First, listen to the examples.

Examples

But my mom said, "_____ have another child."

(**a.**) I am not going to

b. I'm not gonna

Today, _____ talk about only children.

a. we are going to

(**b.**) we're gonna

1. Today, _____ meet two families with only children.

 a. we are going to

 b. we're gonna

2. First, _____ talk with Marion and Mark Carter.

 a. we are going to

 b. we're gonna

3. OK, next, _____ talk to the kids!

 a. I am going to

 b. I'm gonna

4. _____ speak to Marion and Mark's daughter, Tonia.

 a. I'm going to

 b. I'm gonna

5. And this winter, _____ go skiing in Europe.

 a. we are going to

 b. we're gonna

2 Match the phrases in column A and column B to make true sentences about you and the people in your family. (You don't have to use all the phrases in column B.) With a partner, take turns saying your sentences aloud. You can use **going to** or **gonna**. Then share some of your sentences with the class.

(continued on next page)

Example

STUDENT 1: "I'm not *going to* have a big family."

STUDENT 2: "I'm *gonna* travel this year."

A

_____ **1.** I'm (not) going to

_____ **2.** My (wife/husband/best friend) is probably (not) going to

_____ **3.** My (mother/father) is probably (not) going to

_____ **4.** My (brother/sister/cousin) is probably (not) going to

_____ **5.** My parents are (not) going to

B

a. travel this year.

b. have just one child.

c. have a big family.

d. take a vacation this year.

e. have a baby soon.

f. go skiing next winter.

g. get married in a few years.

h. be busy tonight.

SPEAKING SKILL

AGREEING AND DISAGREEING

There are many ways to agree with another person's opinion, and to disagree politely.

Here are some common phrases you can use:

TO AGREE	TO DISAGREE
I agree (with you).	I disagree.
(I think) You're right.	I don't agree (with you).
(I think) That's true.	I don't think that's true. / I don't think so.
That's for sure.	That's not true.

WHEN YOU'RE NOT SURE
I'm not sure about that.
That may be true, but . . .
Maybe . . .

Work in groups of four. Two students will be Group A and two students will be Group B. One student from Group A, read the statement in number 1 that you think is true. Then one student from Group B, use a phrase to agree, disagree, or say you're not sure about Group A's statement. Explain why and state your opinion. Continue taking turns stating opinions and agreeing or disagreeing.

Example

A: Most only children feel very different from their friends.

B: I don't agree. In most big cities, there are lots of only children!

Statements

1. Most only children (*feel / don't feel*) very different from their friends.

2. Only children (*are / are not*) more popular than children with siblings.

3. Only children (*are / are not*) more mature than children with siblings.

4. Many only children (*are / are not*) spoiled.

5. It's (*good / not good*) to be the youngest child in a family.

6. It's (*good / not good*) to be the oldest child in a family.

7. (*All / Not all*) children need siblings.

8. Many only children (*have trouble / don't have trouble*) making friends.

9. It's (*fine / not responsible*) to have more than one child.

10. Children (*need / don't need*) to learn how to enjoy being alone.

■■■■■■■■■■■■■GO TO MyEnglishLab FOR MORE SKILL PRACTICE AND TO CHECK WHAT YOU LEARNED.

FINAL SPEAKING TASK

In this activity, you will role-play a conversation between Matt and Jessica. Matt and Jessica are married. They have a four-year-old daughter named Katie. They are talking about having a second child. Matt is 35 years old. He wants to have another child. Jessica is 34. She isn't sure if another child is a good idea. Try to use the vocabulary, grammar, pronunciation, and language for agreeing and disagreeing from this unit.*

Read about Matt, Jessica, and Katie.

MATT	JESSICA	KATIE
	• apartment: nice but very small • rent: expensive	

• job: engineer for a large company	• job:
	  –day: teaches music in high school
	  –some weekday and weekend evenings: sings at a jazz club
		• spends time with her grandmother or babysitter when Matt and Jessica are working
		• plays with a lot of friends in the neighborhood

• siblings: two brothers, and they're all very close
• thinks it's important to have a sibling
• wants another child
	• siblings: one brother, but they're not very close
	• doesn't think it's important to have a sibling
	• not sure if they should have another child
		• likes to:
		  –read children's books in her room
		  –play with her toys
		  –watch children's videos
		  –play games on the computer

---

* For Alternative Speaking Topics, see page 189.

Follow the steps.

STEP 1: The teacher will divide the class into two groups.

STEP 2: Group A: You are Matt. Make a list of reasons that you want to have another child.

1. _It's important for children to have siblings._

2. _____

3. _____

4. _____

5. _____

6. _____

Group B: You are Jessica. Make a list of reasons that you don't want to have another child.

1. _Siblings aren't always close._

2. _____

3. _____

4. _____

5. _____

6. _____

STEP 3: Work with a partner from the other group. Role-play a conversation between Matt and Jessica. Talk about the future. Use the reasons on your lists. Try to make a decision about having another child.

STEP 4: Share your decisions with the class. How many pairs decided to have another child? How many decided not to have one? Explain your reasons.

Listening Task

Listen to your classmates. Did every role play end the same way? How many pairs made the same decision?

UNIT PROJECT

Learn about family size around the world.

STEP 1: Look online for information about average family size in your country now, 20 years ago, 30 years ago, 40 years ago, and 50 years ago. Then find the same information about a different country.

STEP 2: Draw a graph like the one on page 189 to show how family size has changed (or not changed) in the last 50 years in the two countries.

STEP 3: In class, sit in small groups and explain your information to your classmates. Discuss these questions:

- Did family size change in your country and the other country you learned about? How did it change?

- In your opinion, why did family size change (or stay the same) in your country and the other country you learned about? Try to think of some reasons, and discuss them with your group.

- Think about your parents' families and your family. Are they the same size as the average family in your country? Or is your family bigger or smaller than the average size?

- What do you think?
  In the next 25 or 50 years, what is going to happen to family size in your country and the other country you learned about? Is it going to stay the same, get bigger, or get smaller? Why do you think so?

ALTERNATIVE SPEAKING TOPICS

Discuss one of the topics. Use the vocabulary and grammar from this unit.

1. Look at the graph. What does it show about the number of American families with only one child? Is the same thing happening where you live? Do you know why?

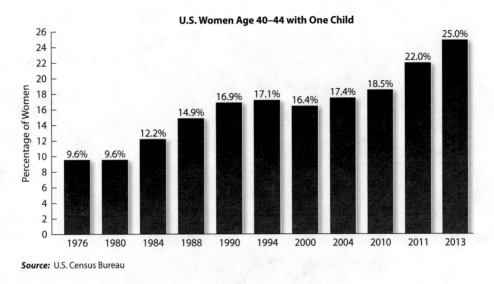

U.S. Women Age 40–44 with One Child

Source: U.S. Census Bureau

2. Do you think it's good to have only one child? Why or why not?

3. How many children do you want to have? (OR: How many children do you have?)

   a. Does your decision have anything to do with the cost of raising a child? (In the U.S., the cost of raising one child for the first 17 years of life is $286,000 – $324,000, before paying for college.)

   b. Does your decision have anything to do with the population explosion[2] in the world?

   c. Do you have other reasons? What are they?

---

[2] **population explosion:** the large increase in the number of people in the world

■ ■ ■ ■ ■ ■ ■ ■ ■ ■ ■ ■*GO TO* MyEnglishLab *TO DISCUSS ONE OF THE ALTERNATIVE TOPICS, WATCH A VIDEO ABOUT BIRTH ORDER AND YOUR HEALTH, AND TAKE THE UNIT 7 ACHIEVEMENT TEST.* ■ ■ ■ ■ ■ ■ ■ ■ ■ ■ ■

SOCCER: THE BEAUTIFUL Game

1 FOCUS ON THE TOPIC

1. Look at the photo. Who is he?

2. What is he doing?

3. Is soccer a popular sport in your country?

GO TO MyEnglishLab TO CHECK WHAT YOU KNOW.

VOCABULARY

1 🎧 Read and listen to a student's presentation about soccer.

Soccer: The world's most popular sport

Soccer is the most popular sport in the world. Outside the U.S., people call it "football," and it's their **favorite** sport. Soccer is easy to learn because the **rules** of the game are **simple**, and the **players** don't need a lot of special things. They just need a ball to **kick** into the goal, and a **field** to play on. With a few friends, anyone can play soccer.

When a player makes a point, people in every country say, "Goal!" *Goal* is an international word. In 2010, the **teams** from Spain and the Netherlands (Holland) played in the final **match** of the World Cup. Spain **won** the match (1–nil). It was their first World Cup! 700 million soccer **fans** all over the world watched the final match on TV.

2 Take turns with a partner. Read the sentences aloud. Choose the correct definition.

1. My **favorite** sport means (*the sport I love the most* / *the most popular sport in my country*).

2. The **rules** of a sport are (*the things you must and must not do* / *the points you get for a goal*).

3. If the rules are **simple**, the game is (*easy* / *difficult*) to understand.

4. The **players** are the people (*in the game* / *watching the game*).

5. When you **kick** a ball, you move it with your (*head / foot*).

6. The **field** is the place where you (*play sports outside / watch the game on TV*).

7. A **team** is a group of people who (*watch / play*) sports together against another group of players.

8. A **match** is a (*game / ball*).

9. My team *won the match* means my team (*scored more goals / played the game*).

10. **Fans** are people who like to (*play / watch*) a sport.

■■■■■■■■■■■■■■■■■■■■■■■■■■■■■■ GO TO MyEnglishLab *FOR MORE VOCABULARY PRACTICE.*

PREVIEW

🎧 Listen to the beginning of a radio show called *The Sports File*. Today's show is about soccer. What will you hear on the show? Check (✓) the items.

_____ opinions of people who love soccer

_____ Americans talking about American football

_____ why soccer is so popular

_____ how to become a professional soccer player

MAIN IDEAS

1 🎧 Listen to the entire radio show. Look again at your answers in Preview above. Were any of your answers correct? Did they help you to understand the radio show?

2 🎧 Listen to the radio show again. Circle the correct answer.

1. The main question that Jane Tuttle wants to answer is _____.

   a. Do Americans love soccer?

   b. Why are so many people watching soccer at Paolinho's?

   c. Why do people from most countries love soccer?

(continued on next page)

2. The four people she talked to are all _____.

    a. soccer fans from around the world

    b. sports fans from the U.S.

    c. soccer players on U.S. teams

DETAILS

Listen again. Check (✓) two correct details about each person on *The Sports File.*

1. Gilberto

_____ **a.** is Brazilian.

_____ **b.** doesn't understand Jane's question.

_____ **c.** thinks soccer is beautiful.

2. Ernesto

_____ **a.** thinks soccer brings people together.

_____ **b.** is very close friends with Anders.

_____ **c.** thinks there are two countries in the world.

3. Anders

_____ **a.** is from Italy.

_____ **b.** thinks people in the U.S. don't understand soccer.

_____ **c.** likes soccer because it is a simple game.

4. Marta

_____ **a.** thinks American football is hard to understand.

_____ **b.** has read books about football.

_____ **c.** thinks soccer is very exciting.

GO TO MyEnglishLab *FOR MORE LISTENING PRACTICE.*

MAKE INFERENCES

UNDERSTANDING COMPARISONS

An inference is a guess about something that is not directly stated. To make an inference, use information that you understand from what you hear.

When people want to explain a difficult idea, they sometimes use a comparison. They say that two things are similar, even though those things may seem very different to you. By thinking about how the two things are similar, you can infer the speaker's meaning.

People often use the phrase "be like" before a comparison. This means "be similar to." (It is **not the same** as the verb *to like*, which means "to enjoy or think something is good.")

> **a. I like** my soccer coach. (I think he's a good coach. I enjoy learning from him.)

> **b. I'm like** my soccer coach. (We have similar personalities. We are the same in some ways.)

🎧 Listen to the example.

Example

Why does Gilberto compare soccer to music?

> **a.** In Brazil, no one really understands why they like soccer or music, so they can't explain it.

> **b.** In Brazil, soccer is not just a game. Soccer is as important as an art, like music.

The correct answer is: **b.** In Brazil, soccer is not just a game. Soccer is as important as an art, like music.

Explanation

Most people enjoy listening to music because it's beautiful or it makes them feel good. People don't need to ask, "Why do you like music?" because the reason is clear.

Most people in Brazil love soccer because it's very exciting and beautiful to watch. Brazilians never ask, "Why do you like soccer?" because almost everyone feels the same way. Gilberto is saying that both music and soccer are very important parts of life in Brazil.

🎧 Listen to the excerpts from the radio show. Choose the best answer to each question. Then discuss your answer with a partner.

Excerpt One

Why does Gilberto say that soccer players are like birds and dancers?

> **a.** because the soccer ball flies through the air very fast

> **b.** because soccer players are very beautiful to watch

(continued on next page)

Excerpt Two

Why does Ernesto say that soccer is like an international language?

    a. because people from many different countries love soccer and can enjoy watching it together.

    b. because people from many different countries all speak English together when they watch a match.

Excerpt Three

Why does Marta say that soccer is not like American football?

    a. American football is more difficult to understand and play.

    b. There are more books about American football.

EXPRESS OPINIONS

1 How do you feel about soccer? On a scale of 1 to 5, where 1 means "not at all" and 5 means "a lot," put an **X** where your opinion is.

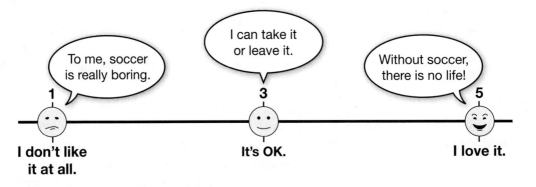

2 Write reasons for your opinion.

1. _____

2. _____

3 In groups of three or four, compare and discuss your opinions.

■ ■*GO TO* MyEnglishLab *TO GIVE YOUR OPINION ABOUT ANOTHER QUESTION.*

COMPREHENSION

America Talks is a radio call-in show in the U.S. Listeners call the show and give their opinions.

🎧 Listen to *America Talks*. Read the sentences. Write **T** (true) or **F** (false). Correct the false information.

_____ **1.** Most American sports fans watched the World Cup.

_____ **2.** Bob thinks Americans prefer sports with high scores.

_____ **3.** Americans like sports that always have a winner.

_____ **4.** America has two traditional sports.

_____ **5.** Drew thinks that the U.S. needs an American soccer superstar.

_____ **6.** David and Victoria Beckham helped a lot of people in the U.S.

_____ **7.** Drew wants Michael Jordan to play American soccer.

VOCABULARY

Fill in the blanks with one of the words from the box. You will not use all the words. Then read the conversation aloud with a partner.

higher	lose	low	score	tie	win

A: Did you see the soccer match yesterday?

B: No. Who won?

A: Korea. The final _____ was 1–0, but there was a 0–0
   1.
_____ for most of the game.
   2.

B: One-nothing! I'm surprised that the final score was so _____.
   3.

A: Yeah, I expected a _____ score. And Italy had a very strong team. I
   4.
didn't expect Italy to _____!
   5.

GO TO MyEnglishLab FOR MORE VOCABULARY PRACTICE.

LISTENING FOR REASONS AND RESULTS

A good listener understands signal words. These are important words that help listeners to understand what kind of information they are going to hear next. Some signal words introduce **reasons**. They tell us *why*. Some signal words introduce **results**. They tell us the *effect* of something else. When you hear the signal words for reasons and results, it will help you to understand what the speaker is going to say next.

Here are three common signal words that introduce **reasons**:

because + [subject + verb]	I love soccer **because** <u>it's exciting</u>.
because of + [noun/noun phrase]	I love soccer **because of** <u>the excitement</u>.
The reason [result] **is that** + [subject + verb]	**The reason** I love soccer **is that** <u>it's exciting</u>.

Here are three common signal words that introduce **results**. When people use these signal words to introduce a **result**, they always say the **reason first**.

(Reason), **so** + *result*	Soccer is exciting, **so** *I love it.*
(Reason.) **That's why** + *result*	Soccer is exciting. **That's why** *I love it.*
(Reason.) **That's (a/the) reason that** + *result*	Soccer is exciting. **That's the reason that** *I love it.*

Listen to this excerpt from the radio talk show and choose the correct answer to the question.

Example

In Bob's opinion, why isn't soccer popular in the U.S.?

    a. The games are slow.

    b. The scores are low.

The correct answer is: **b.** The scores are low.

Explanation

Bob used *because of* to introduce his reason (*the low scores*). He expressed his reason with a noun phrase (no verb).

To express the same reason *with a verb*, you can say, ". . . because *the games have* low scores" or ". . . because *the scores are* low." All of these sentences have the same meaning.

Listen to the excerpts from the radio show. Pay attention to the signal words that introduce reasons and results. Choose the reason or result that each speaker explains.

Excerpt One

In Bob's opinion, why isn't soccer popular in the U.S.?

    a. because Americans don't like their team to lose

    b. because Americans don't like games with tie scores

Excerpt Two

Linda says that most Americans didn't grow up playing and watching soccer. What's the result of this today?

    a. Soccer isn't as popular as other sports in the U.S.

    b. American soccer teams aren't on TV.

Excerpt Three

In Drew's opinion, why isn't soccer popular in the U.S.?

    a. because Americans don't love big soccer superstars

    b. because there aren't any American superstar soccer players

GO TO MyEnglishLab *FOR MORE SKILL PRACTICE.*

CONNECT THE LISTENINGS

STEP 1: Organize

Write the number of each sentence in the correct column. Use the information from Listening One and Listening Two. The first one has been done for you.

1. People from all countries can understand the rules of soccer.

2. Soccer is an art.

3. Most adults in the U.S. never learned to play soccer well.

4. People can play soccer without a lot of expensive things.

5. Soccer doesn't have high scores.

6. Americans have other traditional sports.

7. Soccer sometimes ends in a tie.

(continued on next page)

8. There are no soccer stars from the U.S.

9. Soccer brings people from many countries together.

10. People in the U.S. did not grow up watching soccer on TV.

<table>
<tr><th>WHY SOCCER IS POPULAR
IN MOST COUNTRIES</th><th>WHY SOCCER IS NOT POPULAR
IN THE U.S.</th></tr>
<tr><td>1</td><td></td></tr>
<tr><td></td><td></td></tr>
<tr><td></td><td></td></tr>
<tr><td></td><td></td></tr>
<tr><td></td><td></td></tr>
<tr><td></td><td></td></tr>
<tr><td></td><td></td></tr>
</table>

STEP 2: Synthesize

Role-play with a partner. Student A is from France, and Student B is from the U.S. Student A, explain to Student B why soccer is a great sport. Student B, explain to Student A why many Americans don't like soccer. Use all the information from Step 1: Organize. Each student should add at least five more lines to the conversation. Begin like this:

A: I heard that most Americans don't like soccer. Is that true?

B: Yes, it is.

A: Why? Soccer is so easy to understand.

B: Well, one reason is that . . .

A: . . .

B: . . .

GO TO MyEnglishLab *TO CHECK WHAT YOU LEARNED.*

VOCABULARY

REVIEW

Work with a partner. Two answers are correct. Cross out the **incorrect** word or phrase. Then take turns reading the sentence aloud with the two correct answers. The first one has been done for you.

1. After their team won, the fans (*were very excited / had a party / ~~scored a goal~~*).

   STUDENT A: After their team won, the fans were very excited.

   STUDENT B: After their team won, the fans had a party.

2. Real Madrid is my favorite team. (*I can take them or leave them. / They're the best! / I love them.*)

3. No one is in front of the goal! The player can (*take it / kick the ball in / score a goal*).

4. Let's leave when this (*study / tennis / soccer*) match is over.

5. The goalie is the only (*player /team/ person*) who can use his or her hands.

6. The score was (*14 to 2 / three–nothing / almost finished*).

7. Don doesn't like ties because (*nobody wins / you don't know who is best / you can't watch those games*).

8. In basketball and baseball, the scores are (*not very important / higher than in soccer / never a tie*).

9. It's important to follow the rules in (*television / soccer / school*).

10. You play soccer and (*baseball / basketball / American football*) on a field.

1 Read sentences **A, B,** and **C.** Then choose the correct definition for each **boldfaced** word.

A. In sports, **athletes compete against** their **opponents** and try to **defeat** them.

    1. Athletes are _____.

      a. the players in sports   **b.** superstars

    2. When you **compete against** a team, you _____ a game or sport with them.

      a. play   **b.** win

    3. If you **defeat** the other team, you _____ the game.

      a. win   **b.** lose

    4. Your **opponents** are the players on _____ team.

      a. the other   **b.** your

B. When basketball players **throw** the ball into the basket, they usually **score** two points.

    5. When you **throw** the ball, you put it in the air with your _____.

      a. hand   **b.** foot

    6. If you **score** points, your team _____ them.

      a. loses   **b.** gets

C. In soccer, only the goalies can **catch** the ball. Their job is to **block** the other team's goal.

    7. When you **catch** a ball, you get it with your _____.

      a. hands   **b.** feet

    8. When you **block** a goal, you _____ it.

      a. stop   **b.** win

The Los Angeles Lakers vs. the Phoenix Suns. Final score: Lakers 91, Suns 85.

The U.S. vs. Japan at the 2008 Beijing Olympics. Final score: U.S. 1, Japan 0.

2 Talk about the photos. What is happening in the two photos? Use the vocabulary from Expand (sentences A, B, and C) to explain what is happening. With a partner, write three sentences to share with the class.

Example

The LA Lakers are competing against the Phoenix Suns.

1. _____

2. _____

3. _____

CREATE

Work in groups of three. Look at the list of activities.

- cheerleading
- poker
- eating contests
- wrestling
- extreme skateboarding
- gymnastics

Discuss these questions. Use the vocabulary from Review and Expand.

What is a sport? Are all of these activities sports? Why or why not?

When you have finished, form new groups and have another conversation.

cheerleading   skateboarding

You may begin like this:

Example

A: I think a sport is a game with two teams, a ball, and a goal.

B: I disagree. Tennis and cheerleading don't have a goal.

C: Is cheerleading a sport? Cheerleaders are not **athletes**.

■■■■■■■■■■■■■■■■■■■■■■■■■■■■■■■■■■■GO TO MyEnglishLab FOR MORE VOCABULARY PRACTICE.

GRAMMAR

1 Look at the sentences and answer the questions.

JANE: The world is getting **smaller**.

MARTA: Soccer is **simpler**—and it's also **more exciting** to watch.

BOB: I think Americans like sports with **higher** scores.

LINDA: I think the main reason soccer is **less popular** here is that we just didn't grow up with it.

DREW: David Beckham made Americans **more interested** in soccer.

1. Which adjectives end with -**er**? _____, _____, and _____.

   How many syllables do they have? _____ or _____

2. Which adjectives have *more* or *less* in front of them (and no -**er**)?

   _____, _____, and _____

   How many syllables do they have? _____

COMPARATIVE ADJECTIVES

1. Use the comparative form of adjectives + *than* to compare two people, things, or places.	Soccer is **faster** than baseball.
	Soccer is **more popular** than American football.
If there is a noun after the adjective, use: **a(n)** + *comparative adj.* + *noun* + **than**	Soccer is *a more popular sport* than baseball.
If there are two comparative adjectives connected by **and**, use **than** after the second adjective.	Soccer is **faster** and **more popular** *than* baseball.
Sometimes, it's *not necessary* to mention the second thing in the comparison because it's very clear. In this case, you can omit **than**.	The world is **smaller**. (= than in the past)
2. If an adjective has **one syllable** (e.g., small, big, low, high, fast), add -**er** to the adjective.	Baseball games are **longer than** soccer matches.

(continued on next page)

3. If an adjective has:

two syllables and ends with -e (e.g., *simple*) add **-r** to the adjective.	The rules of soccer are **simpler than** the rules of American football.
two syllables and ends with -y (e.g., *easy, lucky*) change the **y** to **i** and add **-er** to the adjective.	The rules of soccer are **easier than** the rules of American football.

4. For all other **two-syllable adjectives**, and for **adjectives with three or more syllables**, add *more* or *less* before the adjective.	Soccer is **more exciting than** baseball. Soccer is **less popular** in the U.S. **than** in all other countries.

5. The adjectives **good** and **bad** have irregular comparative forms: **good – better than** **bad – worse than**	 My team is **better than** your team this year. Last year, we were **worse** than your team.

2 Complete the sentences. Use the comparative form of the adjective (in parentheses). In some blanks, you do **not** need to use **than**. The first one has been done for you.

Is Soccer Becoming More Popular in the U.S?

Most Americans love baseball, football, and basketball. Soccer is still

<u>less popular than</u> these traditional American sports. However, soccer is slowly
    1. (popular)

becoming _____ in the U.S. The U.S. has many immigrants[2] from
       2. (popular)

other countries. Most of these immigrants grew up with soccer, and they still love

it. They play soccer and they watch international matches on TV. Their interest

in soccer is one reason that Americans are becoming _____ in
         3. (interested)

the sport. In 2010, 24.3 million Americans watched the final match of the World

Cup on television. This number is 41 percent _____ the number
         4. (high)

of Americans who watched it in 2006. This shows that many Americans are

_____ about soccer now.
    5. (excited)

---

[2]**immigrants:** people who leave their native country to live in a new country

Mia Hamm—American women's soccer champion

Mia Hamm is the best women's soccer player in U.S. history. When she was young, she was always very good at sports. She was a _____
6. (good)
athlete _____ most of the boys her age. Mia loved to compete against boys who were _____ and _____
7. (old)   8. (fast)
she was. This made her a _____ athlete. But when she got
9. (strong)
_____, it was _____ for her to play traditional
10. (old)   11. (difficult)
sports like baseball or football. In most American schools, those sports were only for boys. At that time, women's soccer was new in the U.S., so it was

_____ for an American girl to play soccer than other American
12. (easy)
sports. Mia played soccer in high school and she joined the U.S. women's national soccer team when she was only 15 years old. She was _____ all of
13. (young)
the other women on the team. At university, Mia was the "Player of the Year" for three years because she was _____ all of her teammates.
14. (successful)

(continued on next page)

In 1991, when she was 19, Mia competed in her first World Cup (in China).

The U.S. played against teams from Sweden and Brazil. Those teams were

_____ the American team, but the Americans, with Mia Hamm,
        15. (strong)
defeated Sweden (3–2) and Brazil (5–0). Then, the U.S. played against Japan. This

match was _____ the first two, and the U.S. won 3–0. The next
              16. (easy)
match against Taiwan was _____ the match against Japan, and
                          17. (exciting)
the U.S. won with a _____ score (7–0). Then they played in the
                     18. (high)
semi-finals against Germany. The German team was _____ all of
                                                  19. (strong)
the other opponents, but the U.S. team defeated them 5–2. In the final match,

the U.S. competed against Norway, and again, the U.S. team won the match, but

the score was _____ (2–1).
              20. (close)

Mia Hamm played soccer for the U.S. team for 17 years. She competed in four

World Cups and three Olympics. Mia Hamm scored a total of 158 international

goals. That is more than any male or female soccer player in the world. Mia

wants young girls to become _____ in sports. After winning a
                            21. (interested)
gold medal in the Olympics, Mia said, "I hope all you young girls see your[selves]

up there [standing with the winners]. We were just like you." Because of Mia

Hamm and her teammates, many young American women love soccer and

sports.

GO TO MyEnglishLab FOR MORE GRAMMAR PRACTICE.

EMPHATIC AND CONTRASTIVE STRESS

Sometimes we want to show that one word is more important than all the other words in our sentence. To do this, we stress the important word **more than** the other stressed words in the sentence. We say it **louder**, **longer**, and with a **higher pitch** or note.

This word may be important because it:

    a. gives new or surprising information (*emphatic* stress) or

    b. corrects a mistake or gives information that is different from the sentence before it. (*contrastive* stress)

🎧 Listen to how the most important words sound with extra stress and read the explanation.

Example

DAD: **Maya, get** your **SOC**cer ball. (normal stress on the *name, main verb,* and *noun*)

MAYA: I **HAVE** it. (**extra** stress on **HAVE**, even though this verb is not usually stressed. Dad thinks she **doesn't have** her soccer ball, but in fact, she **has** it. She is correcting his information.)

               But I **can't find** my **WA**ter bottle. (normal stress on negative verb; **extra** stress on **WATER**. Maya is contrasting two things: She has her **SOCCER ball**, but she doesn't have her **WATER bottle**.)

1 🎧 Listen to the conversations. Then listen again and repeat each line. Be sure to pronounce the most important words with **extra** stress. Then practice with a partner. Take turns reading the lines for **A** and **B**.

  1. A: SAMMY MADE a GOAL.

     B: He made **THREE** GOALS.

  2. A: I'm TIRED of BASEBALL.

     B: So WATCH the **SOC**CER MATCH today.

  3. A: I WATCH soccer, but I DON'T **PLAY** it.

     B: **TRY** to PLAY it. It's FUN.

  4. A: The JAPANESE team is VERY GOOD.

     B: Yeah. They WON the **A**SIA CUP a few YEARS ago.

(continued on next page)

5. A: SOCCER'S VERY POPULAR here.

B: Yeah. EVERYONE **LOVES** it.

6. A: WHAT KIND of SHOES are you **LOOKING** for?

B: I NEED to BUY **RUNNING SHOES.**

2 Work with a partner. First, read the sentences and explanations together and decide which words should be stressed the most (louder, longer, and higher pitch). Then take turns. Read sentence **a** or **b** aloud. Do not read the explanation in parentheses aloud. Your partner will tell you if you are saying **a** or **b**. Tell your partner if she/he is correct.

1. a. I don't really like watching sports on TV. (But I like watching other programs.)
   b. I don't really like watching sports on TV. (But I like watching sports live.[3])

2. a. All kids need to play sports. (not just a few kids)
   b. All kids need to play sports. (But they usually don't.)

3. a. Zizou got kicked out of[4] the World Cup final! (That's the most important game of all!)
   b. Zizou got kicked out of the World Cup final! (Oh no! He was one of France's best players!)

4. a. Players usually play for their home countries in the World Cup. (but not for other competitions)
   b. Players usually play for their home countries in the World Cup. (not on another country's team)

---

[3] **watching sports live:** watching the players in a stadium or sports arena
[4] **got kicked out of:** was told to leave

3 Work with a partner. Student A, read the first question aloud. Be careful to pronounce the word in **BOLD CAPITAL** letters with EXTRA stress. Student B, cover the questions with a piece of paper. Listen carefully for the most stressed word in the question. Choose the response that has the most stress on the new or different information. Pronounce the response with correct stress. Change roles after Question 3.

<table>
<tr><td><u>Student A Questions</u></td><td><u>Student B Answers</u></td></tr>
<tr><td>1. In American high schools, do girls play **BASEBALL**?</td><td>a. No, girls play **SOFT**BALL
b. No, **GIRLS** play softball.</td></tr>
<tr><td>2. In American high schools, do **GIRLS** play baseball?</td><td>a. No, **BOYS** play baseball.
b. No, girls don't **PLAY** baseball.</td></tr>
<tr><td>3. Is soccer very **POPULAR** where you live?</td><td>a. Yes, **SOCCER** is the most popular sport.
b. Yes, soccer is the **MOST** popular sport.</td></tr>
<tr><td>(*Switch roles.*)</td><td>(*Switch roles.*)</td></tr>
<tr><td>4. What **OTHER** sports are popular in your country?</td><td>a. **BASKET**BALL is very popular in my country.
b. Basketball is very **POP**ULAR in my country.</td></tr>
<tr><td>5. What **SPORTS** did you play when you were a child?</td><td>a. When I was a child, I played **BASKET**BALL and **SOC**CER.
b. When I was a **CHILD**, I played basketball and soccer.</td></tr>
<tr><td>6. Do you play any sports **NOW**?</td><td>a. No, I don't have enough **TIME** to play sports.
b. No, I don't have enough time to **PLAY** sports.</td></tr>
</table>

SPEAKING SKILL

EXPLAINING REASONS AND RESULTS

It's often important to explain to other people **why** we feel a certain way, or why we are doing something. In speaking, the most common ways to introduce **reasons** are *because* and *because of*.

Results are things that happen because of other things. For example, a student who studies a lot will usually get good grades. The good grades are a **result** of studying a lot. To explain results clearly, a speaker can use the signal words *so* and *That's why*.

[result]   [reason]
I always watch the Olympics **because** the athletes are amazing.

[result]   [reason]
I always watch the Olympics **because of** the amazing athletes.

[reason]   [result]
The athletes are amazing, **so** I always watch the Olympics.

[reason]   [result]
The athletes are amazing. **That's why** I always watch the Olympics.

Nicole found a list of Winter Olympic sports in the newspaper. She made notes about what she wants to watch on TV and what she doesn't want to watch.

Look at the list. With a partner, discuss which sports she is going to watch and which sports she isn't going to watch. Explain her reasons. Write at least six sentences. Use **because**, **because of**, **so**, and **That's why**. Then share some of your sentences with the class.

The Winter Olympic Games are coming!

Events will include:

✓ Speed skating — *fast & fun!*
want to see Apolo Ohno!

NO! Figure skating — *on TV too late at night*

✓ Slalom skiing — *makes me remember my racing days!*

NO! Downhill skiing — *too scary!*
don't like to see crashes

✓ Ice hockey — *always fun*

NO! Bobsled — *makes me laugh!*

NO! Cross-country skiing — *not interesting*

bobsledding

speed skating

downhill skiing

Examples

Nicole is going to watch speed skating **because** it's fast and fun.

Nicole is going to watch speed skating **because of** Apolo Ohno.

Speed skating is fast and fun, **so** Nicole is going to watch it.

Nicole wants to see Apolo Ohno. **That's why** she's going to watch speed skating.

1. _____

2. _____

3. _____

4. _____

5. _____

6. _____

■ ■ ■ ■ ■ ■ ■ ■ ■ ■ *GO TO* MyEnglishLab *FOR MORE SKILL PRACTICE AND TO CHECK WHAT YOU LEARNED.*

FINAL SPEAKING TASK

In this activity, you will make and present a 30-second TV commercial for an important soccer match. It is going to be on TV in the U.S. next week.

In the U.S., famous athletes "sell" sports. For example, basketball was not very popular in the U.S. until Michael Jordan became famous. He made it popular. Also, Mia Hamm made women's soccer more popular in the U.S. Many Americans watch football or baseball because they like to see their favorite players.

You are a famous soccer player, and you want Americans to watch the important soccer match next week. Use the vocabulary, grammar, word stress, and language for introducing reasons and results from this unit.*

Presentation

STEP 1: Make notes for your presentation.

a. Think about your message. What is your main point going to be? TV commercials are very short, so you need to give a clear message in a short time. Write the main message in one sentence. (For example, "The **whole world** is watching soccer—**YOU** should watch it, too!") Remember: stressed words can help to make your message stronger.

b. Look back over the unit and choose one or two reasons to support your message. You can also use reasons that are not in the unit.

c. Make notes about the reason that you want to present. Just write down some key words. Do not write out all of the sentences that you will say. Try to speak naturally from your notes. Remember to look at your classmates when you speak. Don't look at your paper.

STEP 2: Practice your commercial with a partner. As you listen to each other, think about these questions:

a. Is the message clear?

b. Did the speaker use stressed words to make the message clear?

c. What are the reasons to watch the soccer match on TV?

d. In your opinion, will people watch the soccer match because of this commercial?

---

* For Alternative Speaking Topics, see page 216.

STEP 3: Discuss one or two ways to improve the presentation.

STEP 4: Perform your commercial for the class (or record it on video).

STEP 5: a. After you watch your classmates' commercials, answer the question below on a piece of paper. Do not write your name. Give the paper to the presenter when he or she is finished.

Name of presenter: _____

What was the main message? _____

b. After all the students have presented, vote on your favorite commercial.

c. Read your classmates' notes to you. Was your message clear? How could you make it better?

UNIT PROJECT

Famous international players in American sports

Many American sports teams have (or had) players from different countries.

STEP 1: Find information online about **one** of these famous international athletes in American sports:

David Beckham	Yao Ming
Miguel Cabrero	Alex Ovechkin
Yu Darvish	Pele
Pau Gasol	Ricky Rubio
Hideki Matsui	Ichiro Suzuki

Answer these questions. Write very short answers on an index card.

1. What country does he come from?

2. What sport does/did he play?

3. What U.S. team does/did he play for?

4. Why is/was he famous?

5. Is he famous in his native country?

6. Did he win any prizes or awards?

7. Any other interesting information

STEP 2: Prepare a short presentation about the player you chose. Practice at home: Sit in front of a mirror. Look at your card, and then look at the mirror and speak. You may look at your card as often as you want, but when you speak, be sure to look at the mirror. This will help you to look at your classmates when you speak in class.

STEP 3: Sit in a small group with students who have information about different athletes. Take turns giving your presentations. Use your notes, but be sure to look at your classmates when you speak.

Listening Task

Listen to your classmates' presentations. Ask for more information.

ALTERNATIVE SPEAKING TOPICS

Discuss one of the topics. Use the vocabulary and grammar from this unit.

1. Many people say that basketball and soccer are similar games. Do you agree? Compare these two sports. How are they similar? How are they different?

2. What sports are popular in the country where you grew up? Did you play any of these sports? If yes, which ones? Were you a good athlete? If you didn't play any sports, why not? How did you spend your free time?

3. "It is more difficult to stay on top than to get there."—Mia Hamm
What does this mean? Do you agree with Mia Hamm's opinion? Explain why or why not.

■■■■■■■■■■■■■■■*GO TO* MyEnglishLab *TO DISCUSS ONE OF THE ALTERNATIVE TOPICS, WATCH A VIDEO ABOUT SPORTS FOR NON-JOCKS, AND TAKE THE UNIT 8 ACHIEVEMENT TEST.* ■■■■■■■■■■■■

UNIT WORD LIST

The **Unit Word List** is a summary of key vocabulary. Words with an asterisk (*) are on the New General Service List (2013) and words with two asterisks (**) are on the AWL (and the NGSL).

UNIT 1

anything* else*
application*
at first*
became*
culture**
foreign*
have problems* (+
  -ing)

host* family*
interested* in
international*
make* friends*
spend* time*
stay*
travel*
warm* (= friendly)

UNIT 2

control*
cut*
draw*
expensive*
inside*
last (vb)*
material*
nature*
outside*

part* of
put* together*
sculpture
space*
specific**
throw* away*
unusual*

UNIT 3

appreciate
breath
cool
good luck charm
mind
modern
pack rat
pass it down

peaceful
popular
protect
sentimental value
style
temporary
traditional

UNIT 4

advice*
afraid*
come up with
completely* new*
creative**
creativity** (only
  AWL)
employees*
exciting*

experience*
for* the first* time*
increase*
make* (you) feel*
  (+ adj)
make* mistakes*
owner*
successful*

(continued on next page)

UNIT 5

a serious issue
be angry with
be in danger
believe in yourself
calm down
come on
confused
give up
hurt

fear
just kidding
keep going
not your fault
shake
still
what's wrong with
    me?

UNIT 6

amazing*
careful*
challenge**
dangerous*
decide*
(be) determined*
discover*
distance*

prove* something*
reach* (one's) goal**
set* a record*
strong*
take* a risk*
unfortunately*
without*

UNIT 7

act*
alone*
can('t)* afford*
get* married*
have a baby*/child*
have* fun*
lonely
make* a decision*
make* money*

mature**
opportunities*
personal*
population*
raise*
responsible*
sibling
take care* of

UNIT 8

fans*
favorite*
field*
higher*
kick*
lose*
low*
match*

players*
rules*
score (n)*
simple*
team**
tie*
won*

GRAMMAR BOOK REFERENCES

NorthStar: Listening and Speaking Level 1, Third Edition	Focus on Grammar, Level 1, Fourth Edition	Azar's Basic English Grammar, Fourth Edition
Unit 1 Present and past tense of *Be*	**Unit 3** Present of *Be*; statements **Part III** *Be*: Past	**Chapter 1** Using *Be* **Chapter 3** Using the Simple Present **Chapter 8** Expressing Past Time, Part 1
Unit 2 Simple present tense	**Part V** Simple Present	**Chapter 3** Using the Simple Present
Unit 3 Simple present tense with Adverbs of frequency	**Unit 14** Simple Present with Adverbs of frequency	**Chapter 3** Using the Simple Present
Unit 4 *There is / There are,* *There was / There were*	**Unit 27** *There is / There are*	**Chapter 5** Talking About the Present 5–4, 5–5
Unit 5 Simple past tense	**Part VIII** Simple Past	**Chapter 8** Expressing Past Time, Part 1 **Chapter 9** Expressing Past Time, Part 2
Unit 6 Present progressive	**Part VI** Present Progressive	**Chapter 4** Using the Present Progressive
Unit 7 Future tense—*be going to*	**Part XI** Future with *Be going to*	**Chapter 10** Expressing Future Time, Part 1 10–1
Unit 8 Comparative adjectives	**Unit 29** Comparative Adjectives	**Chapter 15** Making Comparisons

AUDIOSCRIPT

UNIT 1: A World of Friends

Listening One, page 6, Preview

RECORDING: Hello. This is the Friendship Force. The Friendship Force helps people make friends all over the world. We think, "A world of friends is a world of peace." For more information about the Friendship Force, press 1. To speak with someone about Friendship Force international groups, press 2.

RICK: Hello, Friendship Force. Rick speaking.

NINA: Hi, umm . . . my name is Nina Rodriguez, and I'm interested in the Friendship Force.

RICK: Great!

NINA: But, um, I have some questions.

RICK: Sure, what do you want to know, Nina?

page 7, Main Ideas

RECORDING: Hello. This is the Friendship Force. The Friendship Force helps people make friends all over the world. We think, "A world of friends is a world of peace." For more information about the Friendship Force, press 1. To speak with someone about Friendship Force international groups, press 2.

RICK: Hello, Friendship Force. Rick speaking.

NINA: Hi, umm . . . my name is Nina Rodriguez, and I'm interested in the Friendship Force.

RICK: Great!

NINA: But, um, I have some questions.

RICK: Sure, what do you want to know, Nina?

NINA: Well, first, can college students be in the Friendship Force?

RICK: Sure. We have people of all ages—teenagers, college students, even grandparents!

NINA: Oh, that's great. And, how many people travel together?

RICK: Each group usually has between 15 and 30 people. And each group is from the same city. So everyone can make friends before they go to the new country.

NINA: That's a good idea.

RICK: Uh-huh. But you know, you don't all stay together in the new country. Each person stays with a different host family, you know, in their home.

NINA: Yeah, I understand that.

RICK: OK, good. Because Friendship Force visitors never stay in hotels.

NINA: Oh, that isn't a problem for me. I think living with a family is the best way to learn about a country.

RICK: OK, then. So, what country do you want to go to?

NINA: Well, I'm really interested in Thailand.

RICK: Oh, Thailand is a beautiful country.

NINA: But what about the language? I only speak English.

RICK: Oh, that isn't a problem. Some host families speak English or other languages. But Friendship Force visitors and host families always become good friends.

NINA: Really? Even if they don't speak the same language?

RICK: Language isn't so important! They always understand each other. You'll see!

NINA: OK, that's good. Umm . . . I just have one more question.

RICK: OK.

NINA: Do the visitors have any time to travel around the country?

RICK: Yes, they do.

NINA: Oh, good.

RICK: Most visitors spend one or two weeks with their host family first. And then, after that, they usually travel and see the country. But you know, at the Friendship Force, we say, "People, not places" . . .

NINA: I like that!

RICK: . . . because we think making new friends is the most important thing when you travel.

NINA: I think so, too!

RICK: Good. Any more questions?

NINA: No, I think that's it. Oh—where can I get an application?

RICK: There's an application on our website.

NINA: OK, wow . . . I'm really excited about the Friendship Force! Thank you so much for your help.

RICK: You're welcome, Nina. And good luck.

NINA: Thanks.

RICK: OK, bye now. Take care.

NINA: Bye.

page 8, Make Inferences

Example

NINA: Well, first, can college students be in the Friendship Force?

RICK: Sure. We have people of all ages—teenagers, college students, even grandparents!

NINA: Oh, that's great.

Excerpt One

RICK: But you know, you don't all stay together in the new country. Each person stays with a different host family, you know, in their home.

NINA: Yeah, I understand that.

RICK: OK, good. Because Friendship Force visitors never stay in hotels.

NINA: Oh, that isn't a problem for me.

Excerpt Two

NINA: I'm really interested in Thailand.

RICK: Oh, Thailand is a beautiful country.

NINA: But what about the language? I only speak English.

Excerpt Three

NINA: Do the visitors have any time to travel around the country?

RICK: Yes, they do.

NINA: Oh, good.

RICK: Most visitors spend one or two weeks with their host family first. And then, after that, they usually travel and see the country. But you know, at the Friendship Force, we say, "People, not places"...

NINA: I like that!

Listening Two, page 10, Comprehension

INTERVIEWER: Annie, what were the best things about *Experiment in International Living*?

ANNIE: Well, my group was great! And I loved my host family!

INTERVIEWER: Can you tell us about your group?

ANNIE: Sure. We were all American high school students, but we all came from different states, and we had different religions and cultures.

INTERVIEWER: That's interesting.

ANNIE: Yeah, but you know, we learned that we weren't really so different!

INTERVIEWER: What do you mean?

ANNIE: Well, we spent every day together for four weeks, and we learned that people are people. We *became* such good friends . . . more than friends—we were like a family!

INTERVIEWER: That's wonderful. I'd like to know more about your host family.

ANNIE: Oh, I loved my host family in Costa Rica. They were so *warm* and friendly. They *became* my family, too! From the first day, I felt like I was their daughter. They called me "Ana."

INTERVIEWER: That's so nice. Did you *have any problems speaking* with them?

ANNIE: No, not really. They spoke only a little English, and *at first,* I didn't speak much Spanish. But I learned a lot of Spanish from them, and in my Spanish class, too. And I also learned that language is not always so important!

INTERVIEWER: What do you mean?

ANNIE: Well, you know, sometimes *a smile* can say more than words.

INTERVIEWER: Well, thanks so much, Annie. Do you want to say *anything else*?

ANNIE: Yes! If you're in high school, and you want to have a great summer, go on the Experiment in International Living! It was the best summer of my life—I'm sure it will be the best summer of your life, too!

INTERVIEWER: Thanks, Annie. That was Annie Quinn, from Philadelphia, Pennsylvania. High school students, you can travel with *Experiment* in the summer for 3, 4, or 5 weeks. Groups go to 27 different countries. You can study a foreign language, history, culture, dance, sports—almost anything! Please see the *Experiment* website for more information, or for an application.

page 12, Listening Skill

Excerpt One

ANNIE: My group was great, and . . .

My group was great and I loved my host family.

Excerpt Two

ANNIE: We were all American high school students, but . . .

We were all American high school students, but we all came from different states.

Excerpt Three

ANNIE: They spoke only a little English, and . . .

They spoke only a little English, and at first, I didn't speak much Spanish.

UNIT 2: Making Unusual Art

Listening One, page 34, Main Ideas

MUSEUM GUIDE: Hi, welcome to the museum.

MAGAZINE WRITER: Thanks. I'm very interested in Mia Pearlman's art.

GUIDE: Well, let me tell you a little about her.

WRITER: OK.

GUIDE: Mia is very interested in the world we live in. And she was always interested in the world—even when she was a little girl.

WRITER: [*Laughing*] Really? What do you mean?

GUIDE: Well, for example, when little girls play with dolls, like Barbie dolls, they usually make up stories about them, right?

WRITER: Sure.

GUIDE: But when Mia played with her dolls, she didn't do that. She was only interested in making the place where Barbie lived.

WRITER: You mean, like a Barbie house?

GUIDE: No, it was bigger than a house. It was a really big **space**—like a "Barbie world."

WRITER: That's very **unusual**!

GUIDE: [*Laughing*] Yes, Mia is an **unusual** person! Even when she was a child, she understood: the world is very big, and people are just a *very small* **part of** it.

WRITER: So, is that why her **sculptures** are so big?

GUIDE: Yes. Each **sculpture** is like a little "world."

WRITER: A lot of Mia's **sculptures** look like things we see in **nature**—like clouds, or the wind —like different kinds of weather . . .

GUIDE: Yes! Because her art is about the things in the world that are *bigger* than us, things that people don't **control**—like **nature**, the weather, even war . . .

WRITER: Mmmhmm . . .

GUIDE: So when people look at Mia's **sculpture**, she wants them to feel like they're inside something very big, and they're a small **part of** it—just like they're a small **part of** the world.

WRITER: Oh . . .

GUIDE: Let's look at one of Mia's **sculptures**. This **sculpture** is called *Inrush*.

WRITER: It's beautiful.

GUIDE: OK, look up—do you see that window?

WRITER: Uh-huh . . .

GUIDE: The window is closed, but the sculpture *looks like* clouds and wind that are "rushing in" through the window, moving very quickly into this room.

WRITER: Yes, I see . . .

GUIDE: And the sunlight from outside *really* comes through the window, so it's **part of** the **sculpture** too. It gives the **sculpture** light.

WRITER: So, the **sculpture** is like a **part of nature** inside the museum.

GUIDE: Yes, and when you stand near the **sculpture**, you feel like you're a **part of** it too—so you feel like a **part of nature**.

WRITER: I do . . . I feel like I'm standing inside a cloud . . .

GUIDE: Mia wants people to feel things that they can't feel in the real world . . . That's why she makes art.

WRITER: Interesting! I have some **specific** questions about how Mia makes these **sculptures**.

GUIDE: Sure. What would you like to know?

WRITER: Well, when Mia begins a new **sculpture**, how does she decide what kinds of lines to **draw**?

GUIDE: Mia says that she doesn't really decide this. She just **draws** what she feels at that moment.

WRITER: Oh . . . And how many pieces of paper does she **cut**?

GUIDE: For each **sculpture**, she usually cuts thirty to eighty pieces.

WRITER: Wow. And, what's going to happen to this **sculpture** when this show ends? Is it going to a different museum?

GUIDE: No, when this show ends, her sculpture ends, too.

WRITER: [*A little shocked*] What do you mean?

GUIDE: Well, Mia comes to the museum and she takes down all the pieces of paper. And she never makes this **specific sculpture** again.

WRITER: But why? Her **sculptures** are so beautiful! I don't understand . . .

GUIDE: I know. But Mia thinks **sculptures** are just like dances, or theater, or music concerts. You enjoy them, but they don't **last** forever. And that's life, too—everything has an end. That's another thing Mia wants her art to show.

page 35, Make Inferences

Example

GUIDE: Mia is very interested in the world we live in. And she was always interested in the world—even when she was a little girl.

WRITER: [*Laughing*] Really? What do you mean?

GUIDE: Well, for example, when little girls play with dolls, like Barbie dolls, they usually make up stories about them, right?

WRITER: Sure.

GUIDE: But when Mia played with her dolls, she didn't do that. She was only interested in making the place where Barbie lived.

WRITER: You mean, like a Barbie house?

GUIDE: No, it was bigger than a house. It was a really big space—like a "Barbie world."

WRITER: That's very unusual!

Excerpt One

WRITER: And, what's going to happen to this sculpture when this show ends? Is it going to a different museum?

GUIDE: No, when this show ends, her sculpture ends, too.

WRITER: [*A little shocked*] What do you mean?

Excerpt Two

GUIDE: Well, Mia comes to the museum and she takes down all the pieces of paper. And she never makes this specific sculpture again.

WRITER: But why? Her sculptures are so beautiful! I don't understand . . .

Listening Two, page 37, Comprehension

NARRATOR: Gee's Bend, a small, poor town in Alabama, is making big news in the art world. The big news is quilts—beautiful covers for the bed to keep people warm at night. Now these quilts are in museums; these quilts are works of art. They look like paintings by modern artists. The women in Gee's Bend didn't think their quilts were art. They just made the quilts to stay warm. But these women work just like artists. They decide how to **put** all the pieces **together**, always in new and different ways. The quilts are really beautiful—and unusual. Why? Because the people in Gee's Bend don't have much money. They can't buy **expensive** material. So they make their quilts with material from old clothes, like old jeans and shirts.

ELDERLY WOMAN 1: In Gee's Bend, we don't **throw** any clothes **away**—oh no! We use everything in our quilts.

NARRATOR: One woman made a quilt with her husband's old work clothes. They were the only things she had to remember him.

ELDERLY WOMAN 2: After he died, I took all his shirts and pants, and I made a quilt with them to keep him near me. I can't believe that quilt's in a museum now. A museum! Those clothes were old. My husband wore them **outside**, working on the farm, our potato farm.

MIDDLE-AGED WOMAN: I was 17 when my father died, and my Mama said, "Come here and help me cut up all your Daddy's old clothes." I remember they had all these different blue and brown colors: dark colors from **inside** the pockets, and light colors from the **outside**. Those clothes were so old, but she made them look beautiful in that quilt.

ELDERLY WOMAN 1: To make a quilt, you cut the material into pieces, and then you put them all on the floor. You put the pieces this way and that. You see how the colors look together. Then you take another piece, and another. You don't have a plan, really. That's why we call some of these "Crazy Quilts." (*laughs*) You just keep adding and changing the pieces until they all look good together.

Then, the women—your sisters, daughters, granddaughters—we all help to **put** the pieces **together** and make the quilt. Most evenings, we sit together and **sew** the quilt and we sing, and we talk . . .

NARRATOR: In Gee's Bend, the older women teach the younger women to make quilts, and they teach them about their families.

ELDERLY WOMAN 2: My great-grandmother came from Africa. She made a quilt with all the colors of Africa. And when I was very little, every day she said, "Come on now, sit down and eat your lunch on this quilt. Let me tell you my story. Listen to the story of my life."

NARRATOR: Grandmothers teaching granddaughters, mothers teaching daughters—working together for years. In Gee's Bend, a very poor town, the art is rich.

page 39, Listening Skill

Example

. . . these women work just like artists. They decide how to **put** all the pieces **together**, always in new and different ways.

Excerpt One

The quilts are really beautiful—and unusual. Why? Because the people in Gee's Bend don't have much money. They can't buy expensive material. So they make their quilts with material from old clothes . . .

Excerpt Two

So they make their quilts with material from old clothes, like old jeans and shirts. [. . .] One woman made a quilt with her husband's old work clothes.

Excerpt Three

NARRATOR: In Gee's Bend, the older women teach the younger women to make quilts, and they teach them about their family.

ELDERLY WOMAN 2: My great-grandmother came from Africa. She made a quilt with all the colors of Africa. And when I was very little, every day she said, "Come on now, sit down and eat your lunch on this quilt. Let me tell you my story. Listen to the story of my life."

UNIT 3: Special Possessions

Listening One, page 59, Preview

To make a dream catcher, we first use parts of trees and plants to make a circle. It shows how the sun travels across the sky. Next, we make a web with a hole in the center. [. . .] Also, there is a little feather in the center. The meaning of the feather is "breath" or "air."

page 60, Main Ideas

PROFESSOR: Class, today we have a special guest, Mr. George Wolf of the Ojibwe Nation. Please welcome Mr. Wolf. [*Sound of applause*]

GEORGE WOLF: Hello, class. Today, I am happy to tell you the story of dream catchers. This is a story from my Ojibwe people . . . Imagine a time long, long ago. All our people lived together and enjoyed telling our **traditional** stories about Spider Woman—the one who gave life to the world. In our stories, we talked about her beautiful web. Every morning, she made her web to catch the sun for us. Then, we started moving to other parts of North America. As we moved far away, it became difficult for Spider Woman to take care of us all. To help Spider Woman, all of our mothers, sisters, and grandmothers started making dream catchers for sleeping babies. We still make dream catchers today.

To make a dream catcher, we first use parts of trees and plants to make a circle. It shows how the sun travels across the sky. Next, we make a web with a hole in the center. The dream catcher is very important. The web stops bad dreams from entering the mind of the sleeping baby. Only good dreams pass through the hole in the center. This **protects** the baby—keeping out bad dreams, letting in the good dreams. Also, there is a little feather in the center. The meaning of the feather is "**breath**" or "air." As the little feather moves in the air, the baby watches it and feels happy. The baby enjoys good, healthy air.

Now remember, the baby will grow. He or she will not stay a baby forever. This is just like the dream catcher! The dream catcher is **temporary**—it is made of trees and plants, and it does not last. But of course, old traditional ways always change. Today you can find many styles of dream catchers with so many beautiful colors and feathers. These dream catchers are made of **modern** materials. Many people use them and give them as gifts. They believe that the dream catcher will stop bad dreams. The good dreams, the important dreams—all of these come to you through the little hole in the center. In this way, the dream catcher is good for your **mind**. It will help you to feel happy and **peaceful**.

And of course, in the twenty-first century, you can always shop for dream catchers online. [*Laughter*] There is one website that says dream catchers are good gifts for friends. It says that when you give a dream catcher to a friend, other people will start asking, "Where did you get that beautiful dream catcher?" And your friend will tell the story of you and your friendship, and the story of you giving the dream catcher as a gift. Do you see how beautiful this is? The dream catcher helps your friend to remember you, to **appreciate** your love and friendship.

To conclude, I want to say that traditional life is very important to Native Americans. Our young people still learn about our culture today. They understand that dream catchers are important to us. Today, you sometimes see very big dream catchers in stores and online. These are **popular**, but they are not traditional. The traditional size is small—just four or five inches across. *Also*, you sometimes see dream catchers in people's cars. Maybe people think they are good luck for driving. But no, the dream catcher is not for your car. The traditional dream catcher goes over your bed, in the place where you sleep and dream.

Thank you so much for listening today! I wish you all beautiful dreams!

page 62, Make Inferences

Example

The dream catcher is very important. The web stops bad dreams from entering the mind of the sleeping baby. Only good dreams pass through the hole in the center. This protects the baby—keeping out bad dreams, letting in the good dreams.

Excerpt One

The good dreams, the important dreams—all of these come to you through the little hole in the center. In this way, the dream catcher is good for your mind. It will help you to feel happy and peaceful.

Excerpt Two

Your friend will tell the story of you and your friendship, and the story of you giving the dream catcher as a gift. Do you see how beautiful this is?

Excerpt Three

You sometimes see dream catchers in people's cars. Maybe people think they are good luck for driving. But no, the dream catcher is not for your car. The **traditional** dream catcher goes over your bed . . .

Listening Two, page 64, Comprehension

SARA: Is it OK if I put my books over here? How about my computer?

AMBER: That's fine.

SARA: [*A little startled*] Look! There's someone outside with a big toy bear! I mean, it's really big. I can't believe it!

AMBER: Where?

SARA: Outside. She's getting out of the car with her parents. She's coming this way!

AMBER: I see her now. I think the bear is cute! Here— let me help you with that computer . . .

[*Sound of a knock. A door opens, and Lauren enters. Her muffled voice speaks. "Bye, Mom. Bye, Dad. I'll be OK. I'll call you . . ."*]

LAUREN: Hello? Anybody here?

SARA: [*Calling*] Come in.

LAUREN: [*Confidently*] Hi. I'm Lauren.

SARA: I'm Sara, and this is Amber. [*Amber greets Lauren.*]

AMBER: Wow, that's a big bear. And now he's in college with you!

LAUREN: [*Proudly*] She's in college with me. This is Lucy—my special bear. She goes everywhere with me.

AMBER: That's **cool**.

LAUREN: Yeah. Lucy has a lot of **sentimental value**. She was my grandmother's bear *for a long time*. Then my grandmother gave her to my mom, and my mom passed her down to *me*!

SARA: [*Casually*] I guess that's pretty cool—for a toy.

LAUREN: [*A bit defensively*] Lucy isn't just a toy. She's a part of my life—and part of my family, too. What about you? Don't you have any special possessions?

AMBER: *Not really. I'm not a pack rat. I never keep old things.* Old things really aren't that important to me. How about you, Sara?

SARA: I don't know. I don't think about it much. But I do have something special. See this *dream catcher*? I'm going to hang it right over my bed to help me catch *good dreams.*

LAUREN: [*Impressed*] Really? It catches *good dreams*?

SARA: Yes—it's a Native American tradition. It stops the bad dreams. It only lets the good dreams come into your mind. Isn't it beautiful?

LAUREN: Yes, it is. Is it a **good luck charm**? Does it help you pass tests?

SARA: [*Laughing*] No, I use my *lucky pen* for that. When I take notes with my lucky pen, I usually get *A's!* What about you—do you ask the big bear for help with your tests?

LAUREN: No. I just use my big brain for that . . . no help from Lucy on tests!

page 67, Listening Skill

Excerpt One

I'm not a pack rat. I never keep old things.

Excerpt Two

[. . .] See this **dream catcher?** I'm going to hang it right over my bed to help me catch **good dreams**.

Excerpt Three

[. . .] I use my **lucky pen** for that. When I use my lucky pen, I usually get *A's!*

UNIT 4: Creativity in Business

Listening One, page 87, Preview

PROFESSOR CHANDLER: OK, everyone, let's get started. Today, our guest speaker is KK Gregory. KK is a **successful** business **owner**, and she's only seventeen years old. Her company makes Wristies. KK?

KK GREGORY: Hi, . . . umm . . . It's really **exciting** to be here, in a business school class, because *I'm* still in high school! I'm 17 now, but when I started my company, I was 10.

page 88, Main Ideas

PROFESSOR CHANDLER: OK, everyone, let's get started. Today, our guest speaker is KK Gregory. KK is a **successful** business **owner**, and she's only seventeen years old. Her company makes Wristies. KK?

KK GREGORY: Hi, . . . umm . . . It's really **exciting** to be here, in a business school class, because *I'm* still in high

school! I'm 17 now, but when I started my company, I was 10.

STUDENTS' VOICES: That's unbelievable! Wow! So young . . .

KK GREGORY: Really! It's true . . . See? These are Wristies. They're long gloves, but they have no fingers. So they keep your hands and your wrists warm and dry, but you can move your fingers easily. You can wear them outside, for sports or work. But you can also wear them inside, in a cold house or office. There are really a lot of places that you can wear them.

PROFESSOR CHANDLER: That's great. KK, could you tell everyone how you got the idea to make Wristies?

KK GREGORY: Sure. Um . . . As I said, I was 10 years old, and it was winter, and I was playing outside in the snow. I was wearing warm clothes and warm gloves, but my wrists were really cold! And that's when I had the idea. I just thought of it. So I went home and I found some warm material. I put it around my wrists and I made a little hole for my thumb. And that's how I made the first pair of Wristies.

PROFESSOR CHANDLER: That's so interesting. Are there any questions? Yes, Nathan?

STUDENT 1 [MALE]: Yeah, um . . . how did you decide to start a business?

KK GREGORY: Well, at first, I didn't think about starting a business at all. I mean, I was only 10! I just made a lot of Wristies in different colors, and I gave them to my friends. They all wore them every day and loved them, and I was happy! But then my friends said, "You know, you can sell these things!" And I thought, "Hmm . . . that could be exciting!" So, I asked my mother about it, and she thought it was a great idea. And then she helped me to start my company.

PROFESSOR CHANDLER: Really . . . Did your mother have any business **experience**?

KK GREGORY: No! My mother didn't know anything about business, and of course I didn't either. But we talked to a lot of people and we asked a lot of questions, we got a lot of **advice**, and we learned a lot. There were a few problems in the beginning, but most of the time, we had fun!

STUDENT 2 [FEMALE]: KK, where can people buy Wristies?

KK GREGORY: Oh, a lot of department stores and clothing stores sell them, and there's also a website. And one time, I went on a TV shopping show. I was really nervous, but it was so exciting—I sold 6000 pairs of Wristies in 6 minutes!

STUDENTS: Wow! Six thousand pairs . . . That's unbelievable!

KK GREGORY: Yeah, it was! And I had a great time!

PROFESSOR CHANDLER: OK, there are just a few minutes left. Is there one more question? Yes? Marla?

STUDENT 3 [FEMALE]: KK, do you have any advice for us?

KK GREGORY: Advice? Well, there are a lot of things, but I guess the most important thing is to be **creative**. You know, don't **be afraid to** try something new.

PROFESSOR CHANDLER: I think that's great advice, KK. Ms. KK Gregory—thank you so much for speaking to us today. And good luck!

KK GREGORY: Thank you.

page 90, Make Inferences

Excerpt One
KK: I'm **SEVENTEEN** NOW, but WHEN I STARTED MY COMPANY, I was **TEN**.

Excerpt Two
KK: They're LONG **GLOVES**, but they have **NO FINGERS**.

Excerpt Three
You can WEAR them **OUT**SIDE, for SPORTS or WORK. But you can ALSO WEAR them **IN**SIDE, in a COLD HOUSE or OFFICE.

Excerpt Four
I was WEARING **WARM** CLOTHES and **WARM** GLOVES, but my WRISTS were REALLY **COLD**!

Listening Two, page 92, Comprehension

PROFESSOR CHANDLER: OK, everybody . . . what can we learn from KK Gregory? First, she **came up with** a new idea. She made something that SHE needed and OTHER people needed, too. Second, she listened to other people. When her friends said, "You can sell these Wristies," she listened to them. And when she decided to start a business, she went to people with business experience and she asked them for advice. That's important. You have to listen to people. And third, KK wasn't afraid to try something **completely** new. She didn't know anything about business, but she wasn't afraid to start her own company. You see, sometimes children can do great things because they aren't afraid to try, and they aren't afraid to make mistakes. And you know what *our* problem is? We're not children anymore, so we *are* afraid. We're afraid to do new things and creative things because we're afraid to make mistakes! In school, at our jobs, making mistakes is bad, right?

STUDENTS: Yeah, sure, right . . .

PROFESSOR CHANDLER: OK, so then what happens? We don't want to make mistakes, so we stop being creative. We forget that great ideas sometimes come from mistakes! But—and this is very important—we

can learn how to be creative again. We can **increase** our creativity if we can remember how children feel. That's what I want to teach you. Now, how do we do it? Well, today we're going to do it with a relaxation exercise.

STUDENTS: What? A relaxation exercise? Huh? Really?

PROFESSOR CHANDLER: So let's begin. OK, now, everybody close your eyes . . . Everybody! Come on . . . Try to relax . . . relax. Now, think about when you were a child . . . Maybe you were 7, or 10, or 11 . . . Think about a time that you did something new . . . you tried to do something **for the first time** . . . and you weren't afraid . . . You did it . . . and **it made you feel** good . . . Try to remember that good feeling . . . Take your time . . . just think . . . When you remember something, you can open your eyes, and then tell your story to another student. When you're finished, we'll discuss your stories together.

UNIT 5: Understanding Fears and Phobias

Listening One, page 113, Preview
A phobia is a very strong fear. When you have a phobia, your body sometimes shakes and your heart beats very fast. You feel like you are in danger, but really there is no danger.

page 114, Main Ideas

DOCTOR JONES (DJ): Good morning and welcome to PSYCHED. I'm Doctor Jones and this is a show about real life and the human mind. This morning we're going to talk about phobias.

A phobia is a very strong **fear**. When you have a phobia, your body sometimes **shakes** and your heart beats very fast. You feel like you are **in danger**, but really there is no danger. For example, I know one person with arachnophobia, the fear of spiders. She can't even look at a picture of a spider. Now, a picture can't **hurt** you. We all know that. But a phobia means having a very strong fear—when there is really no danger. A phobia is very strong, and it changes your life. Believe me, a phobia is a very **serious issue**.

[*Sound effect indicating a caller*]

DJ: Good morning! Here's our first caller: Anna, from New York. Hello, Anna.

ANNA: [*Excited; high-energy*] Doctor Jones, hello! Thanks so much for taking my call. I have a phobia story for you.

DJ: Please go ahead. We're listening.

A: Well, first of all, I really agree with you—a phobia is a very **serious issue**. Here's my story: I always wanted to go to Paris. So I worked really hard and saved a lot of money. Finally, I went to Paris, and I was so happy. I went to the Eiffel Tower . . . you know, it was the dream of my life. I was so excited when I started to climb up the tower. But after a few minutes, I started to feel very **scared**. I didn't know where I was. And I was **confused**. Where was the top? Where was the bottom? I just didn't know. So I started running down the stairs really fast. I was so **scared**—I had to get out. There were lots of kids on the stairs, kids on a class trip or something. But I didn't care. I just ran past them! I had to get out. I felt like I was going to die in there.

DJ: It sounds like you had claustrophobia: the fear of small spaces. Was that your first experience with a phobia?

A: Yes. And that was just the beginning. Then it got worse: After I came home, I couldn't take elevators or drive my car.

DJ: Yes, because those are both small, closed spaces.

A: For a long time, I couldn't do so many things.

DJ: What kinds of things?

A: Well, some of my good friends live in tall apartment buildings, and I was afraid to take the elevator. I always walked up the stairs—and it took forever! And when I looked for a new job, I could only work in low buildings, not high ones. And I couldn't drive my car, so I couldn't travel easily.

DJ: I see . . . So, there were a lot of changes in your life . . .

A: Yeah, and not good ones. But I'm better now.

DJ: What helped you?

A: Different things—going to doctors. They helped me. And reading books. I read about twenty books a week because I really want to understand my phobias.

DJ: And how's your life today?

A: It's **still** not very easy, but it's better. I'm a lot better with elevators.

DJ: Any advice for people with elevator phobias?

A: Yes—don't take a job in a high building—not even for a million dollars! [*Both laugh*] I'm just kidding. I guess my advice is: don't be angry with yourself. Lots of people have phobias—you're not the only one. And it's not your fault.

DJ: That's right, Anna. I completely agree. Thanks so much for calling today . . . and good luck!

page 116, Make Inferences

Example

ANNA: . . . I had to get out. I felt like I was going to die in there . . .

Excerpt One

ANNA: I always walked up the stairs—and it took forever!

Excerpt Two

ANNA: Different things—going to doctors. They helped me. And reading books. I read about twenty books a week because I really want to understand my phobias.

Excerpt Three

DOCTOR JONES: Any advice for people with elevator phobias?

ANNA: Yes—don't take a job in a high building—not even for a million dollars!

Listening Two, page 118, Comprehension

PSYCHOLOGIST: **Come on**, Allen. You can do it. We talked about this. You **know what to do**.

ALLEN: I know. I know *what* to do, but I just can't do it.

PSYCHOLOGIST: Now what is it, Allen? What exactly are you scared of?

ALLEN: I don't know. I just hate crossing the bridge. I know there is no reason to be afraid—but I just don't want to do it!

PSYCHOLOGIST: **Come on,** Allen. You can do it. Think of all the other things you do well: your job, your sports, your music. You**'re very good at** everything you do. You can do this, too. Remember what the book said? **Believe in yourself**!

ALLEN: [*Mumbling*] Too many trucks.

PSYCHOLOGIST: What did you say?

ALLEN: [*Nearly shouting*] I'm scared of the trucks! The trucks are going to hit me!

PSYCHOLOGIST: They're not going to hit you, Allen. **Calm down.** Don't look at the trucks. Just look at the road.

ALLEN: I can't! This bridge is so high!

PSYCHOLOGIST: Don't think about that, Allen. Just look at the road. Look straight ahead.

ALLEN: Oh no, we're on the bridge! I hate driving—it scares me.

PSYCHOLOGIST: **Keep going**, Allen. Look straight ahead. You're doing fine. **Keep going.** [*Sound of traffic*] There! You did it! You crossed the bridge!

ALLEN: *We* crossed the bridge. I can't do it **by myself. What's wrong** with me? Why am I so afraid of a bridge? Why aren't the books helping me? Why can't you help me?

PSYCHOLOGIST: I *am* helping you, Allen. The books are helping, too. You're going to cross this bridge by yourself. You will. Now keep going . . .

page 120, Listening Skill

Example

ALLEN: I'm scared of the trucks! The trucks are going to hit me!

PSYCHOLOGIST: They're NOT going to hit you, Allen. Calm down.

Excerpt One

PSYCHOLOGIST: You're doing fine. Keep going. There! You did it! You crossed the bridge!

ALLEN: WE crossed the bridge. I can't do it by myself.

Excerpt Two

ALLEN: Why am I so afraid of a bridge? Why aren't the books helping me? Why can't you help me?

PSYCHOLOGIST: I AM helping you, Allen. The books are helping, too You're going to cross this bridge by yourself. You will. Now keep going . . .

UNIT 6: Risks and Challenges

Listening One, page 139, Preview

SUE: Hello again. I'm Sue Fujimura.

JIM: And I'm Jim Goodman.

SUE: And we're speaking to you from a boat, somewhere between Cuba and Key West, Florida. As everyone knows, Diana Nyad is trying for the fourth time to swim from Cuba to Florida. After 51 hours in the ocean, she is still swimming, even though things are not going very well.

page 139, Main Ideas

SUE: Hello again. I'm Sue Fujimura.

JIM: And I'm Jim Goodman.

SUE: And we're speaking to you from a boat, somewhere between Cuba and Key West, Florida. As everyone knows, Diana Nyad is trying for the fourth time to swim from Cuba to Florida. After 51 hours in the ocean, she is still swimming even though things are not going very well right now.

JIM: Yes, as you can hear it's raining very hard and it's very windy.

SUE: Unfortunately the wind is pushing Diana very far off course. And that means she will have to swim much longer to get to Florida.

JIM: She also has jellyfish bites all over her body and they're making her feel very sick.

SUE: Yes, she is swimming slowly now and her body is shaking—and is she having problems breathing?

JIM: I think she is. That's also because of the jellyfish. They are very dangerous. You know, most swimmers give up if they get a few jellyfish bites or if the weather is as…as terrible as it is right now. But, just look at Diana. How does she do it?!

SUE: I know! She really is amazing. You know, long-distance swimming is so difficult. Even in good conditions.

JIM: That's very true. Diana called it the "loneliest sport in the world." I mean she is all alone out there in the ocean for days. It's also difficult because it's boring. She

has to move her body the same way again and again for so many hours. That is really hard.

SUE: It sure is. So I want to tell people how Diana pushes herself to keep going after so many hours and days of swimming. Diana doesn't only train her body, she also trains her mind. Diana knows how to clear her mind, so when she's swimming, she doesn't think about anything.

JIM: How does she do that?

SUE: She does a kind of meditation.[1] When Diana is swimming, she counts from one to 1000 in four different languages: English, French, Spanish, and German. She does that over and over. She also knows a lot of songs. When she finishes counting, she sings those songs in her mind, sometimes one or two thousand times. Can you imagine that? But Diana says that when she counts and sings, she can't think about anything else. And when her mind is clear, she can keep swimming for a long time.

JIM: That's interesting, because scientists say that for long-distance sports, training the mind is more important than training the body. That's probably why Diana said that long-distance swimming "is not a young person's game."

SUE: Right. Older people can train their minds more easily. So even when Diana's having a lot of problems like now, she can keep swimming. She doesn't let the problems stop her.

JIM: To Diana, problems are just challenges, and she likes challenges!

SUE: That's right. People also say that Diana Nyad has no fear. I mean, even though there are sharks in this ocean, she is swimming without a shark cage to protect her! No shark cage! Who does that?!

JIM: [*laughing*] She's really not afraid of anything! And she's so determined! I mean, she's 62 years old, and she's trying to set a new long-distance swimming record for the fourth time! How many people are that determined to do anything?

SUE: I think we can agree that Diana Nyad is much more than an amazing swimmer. Y'know, a lot of people say that because of Diana's example, they chose new goals in their own lives and pushed themselves to reach them.

JIM: Yes, I think many people have learned a lot from Diana, especially older people. She really shows people that it's never too late to have a goal.

SUE: Oh, no! Jim, look . . . Diana is swimming over to her boat.

---

[1] *meditation:* spending time in quiet thought in order to clear your mind or relax.

JIM: She's talking to her coach and doctor.

SUE: Oh, no! They're pulling her out of the water. I hope she's OK . . . We'll be back in just a moment with the latest information on Diana Nyad.

page 140, Make Inferences

Example 1

JIM: You know, most swimmers give up if they get a few jellyfish bites, or if the weather is as . . . as terrible as it is right now. But, just *look at* Diana! *HOW* does she *DO it?!*

SUE: I know! She really is amazing.

Example 2

SUE: So I want to tell people how Diana pushes herself to keep going after so many hours and days of swimming. Diana doesn't only train her body, she also trains her mind. Diana knows how to clear her mind, so when she's swimming, she doesn't think about anything.

JIM: How does she **DO** that?

SUE: She does a kind of meditation.

Excerpt One

SUE: She does a kind of meditation. When Diana is swimming, she counts from one to 1000 in four different languages: English, French, Spanish, and German. She does that over and over. She also knows a lot of songs. When she finishes counting, she sings those songs in her mind, sometimes one or two thousand times. Can you imagine that?

Excerpt Two

SUE: People also say that Diana Nyad has no fear. I mean, even though there are sharks in this ocean, she is swimming without a shark cage to protect her! No shark cage! Who does that?!

Excerpt Three

JIM: She's really not afraid of anything! I mean, she's 62 years old, and she's trying to set a new long-distance swimming record for the fourth time! How many people are that determined to do anything?

Listening Two, page 142, Comprehension

INTERVIEWER: Hi, Jeremy. Thanks for taking some time to meet with me.

JEREMY MANZI: That's OK.

INT: So, tell me . . . why did you decide to go on Outward Bound this summer?

JM: Well, I wanted to have some new experiences and learn how to do some new things. Those were my main goals.

INT: Mmm. And why were those goals important to you? Do you know?

JM: Mmm . . . yeah, I think it's because I'm the youngest kid in my family, so *even though* I'm fourteen, everyone thinks I'm the "baby." So I wanted **to prove** that I'm not.

INT: You wanted **to prove** that to your family?

JM: Yeah, and to myself, too.

INT: And do you feel like you're **proving** that now?

JM: Yeah, definitely. I'm doing a lot of really hard things, and it feels great.

INT: Really? But don't you sleep outside at night, and walk in the mountains with a heavy backpack?

JM: [*Laughs*] I know, yeah, that's a challenge! But all the kids help each other, so *even though* it's hard, we're really having a good time. It's pretty cool!

INT: Yes, it is. So, what kinds of things do you do?

JM: Well, we went whitewater rafting, and we also went rock climbing up this really big mountain . . .

INT: Wow, did you know how to do those things before you came here?

JM: No, and I also didn't think I could do those things, especially the rock climbing. When I saw that mountain, I said, "There's NO WAY I can do that!" [*In a low voice*] I was afraid!

INT: Well—sure!

JM: But after I did it, I felt like, "Wow—I really climbed that mountain!" I was so excited! So, I feel a lot more confident. That's the really cool thing about Outward Bound. You learn that you can do a lot of things *even though* you're afraid.

INT: So, it sounds like you're **discovering** some new things about yourself.

JM: Yeah. Like now, I don't think any challenge is too hard for me, because rock climbing up that mountain was the hardest thing I ever did in my life! Our group leaders say that most people are really **strong** inside, but they just don't know it.

INT: I see, so when you do these difficult things, like rock climbing, you can **discover** how **strong** you really are.

JM: Right. And that's really exciting!

INT: I can understand that. But aren't some of the things you do a little dangerous? Aren't you all a little young to **take** such big **risks**?

JM: No, our group leaders teach us how to do everything, and how to be very **careful**. We always feel safe. So *even though* we're doing difficult things, it's really not dangerous.

INT: Well, you do sound like you've become a very confident young man!

JM: Thank you.

INT: OK, then, Jeremy, thanks, and enjoy the rest of your experience.

JM: Thanks, I will! [*In a faint voice: Hey guys . . . Wait up!*]

page 145, Listening Skill

Example
That's the really cool thing about Outward Bound. You learn that you can do a lot of things even though you're afraid.

Excerpt One
INT: And why were those goals important to you, do you know?
JM: Mmm…yeah, I think it's because I'm the youngest kid in my family, so even though I'm fourteen, everyone thinks I'm the baby.

Excerpt Two
INT: Really? But don't you sleep outside at night, and walk in the mountains with a heavy backpack?
JM: [*Laughs*] I know, yeah, it's a challenge! But all the kids help each other, so *even though* it's hard, we're really having a good time.

Excerpt Three
JM: No, our group leaders teach us how to do everything, and how to be very **careful**. We always feel safe. So *even though* we're doing difficult things, it's really not dangerous.

UNIT 7: Only Child—Lonely Child?

Listening One, page 167, Preview

MARIA SANCHEZ: Hello! Welcome to "Changing Families." I'm Maria Sanchez, and today we're going to talk about only children. In the past, people thought that an only child was a **lonely** child. But now, more and more families all over the world are deciding to **have** just one **child**, especially in big cities. Today, we are going to meet two families with only children. First, we're going to talk with Marion and Mark Carter, from Chicago, Illinois. Hello!

page 168, Main Ideas

MARIA SANCHEZ: Hello! Welcome to "Changing Families." I'm Maria Sanchez, and today we're going to talk about only children. In the past, people thought that an only child was a **lonely** child. But now, more and more families all over the world are deciding to **have** just one **child**, especially in big cities. Today, we are going to meet two families with only children. First, we're going to talk with Marion and Mark Carter, from Chicago, Illinois. Hello!
MARK AND MARION: Hi. Hi, Maria.
MARIA: Welcome! Please tell us—Why did you decide to **have** just one **child**?

MARK: Well, um . . . we were both thirty-six when we **got married** . . .
MARIA: Uh-huh.
MARION: . . . and then, when we **had** Tonia, our daughter, I was thirty-eight. Tonia is so wonderful, and we love her more than anything. But . . . well, it isn't easy **to raise** a young child at our age.
MARK: [*Laughing a little*] That's for sure. We're always tired!
MARIA: I think many *young* parents feel the same way!
MARK: Mmm . . . Maybe . . . Anyway, at some point, we just decided that we couldn't **take care of** Tonia *and* a new baby.
MARION: Yeah. We decided that we were happy with our little family, and that one child was enough for us.
MARIA: Uh-huh. And how does Tonia feel about your family? Is she ever **lonely**?
MARION: Um . . . I don't think so, because we spend a lot of time with her, and she has lots of friends.
MARK: That's for sure! She's very popular!
MARIA: Really! You know, that's interesting because I read that only children are often more popular—and also more intelligent—than children with **siblings**.
MARK: Yes, that IS interesting!
MARIA: Isn't it? It's really something to think about. Another thing to think about is the world **population** problem. By the year 2050, there are going to be more than 9 billion people in the world, and we don't know if we're going to have enough food and water for everyone. So some people feel that it's not **responsible** to have more than one child. They say that everyone needs to think about the future of the world, not just about their own family. Mark, Marion—did you think about that issue, too?
MARK: Well, of course we know about the **population** problem in the world, and we think it's a very serious issue, but I'd say that our **decision** was really a **personal** one.
MARIA: I understand. OK, thank you, Mark and Marion. And now, let's say hello to Tom and Jenna Mori from New York City.
TOM AND JENNA: Hi. Hi, Maria!
MARIA: Now, Tom and Jenna, you also **made a decision** to **have** only one **child**.
TOM: Yes, that's right . . .
MARIA: Can you tell us why?
TOM: Well, it was a difficult **decision** for us . . .
JENNA: Yes, very difficult . . .
TOM: . . . because Jenna and I really love kids. When we got married, we wanted to have two or three children.
MARIA: Oh?
JENNA: But we're both teachers, and I'm sure you know, teachers don't **make a lot of money**!

MARIA: That's true. Most teachers aren't rich!

JENNA: Well, *before* we **had** a **child**, money wasn't really so important to us.

MARIA: That's interesting . . .

JENNA: But *now* . . . well, when you **have a child**, it's *different*. We want our son Jay to have a good life—you know—to go to a good school, take piano lessons, travel . . . And those things are very expensive!

MARIA: You're right about that!

TOM: Yeah, and we know we **can't afford** all of those things for *two* children. So we decided to **have** only one **child**, so we can give him the best.

MARIA: I understand. But do you think Jay wants a **sibling**? Does he ever feel **lonely**?

TOM: Jay?! Never!

JENNA: Oh, no. He's always so busy with his friends.

TOM: Yeah, and with his sports and his music, too.

MARIA: Well, that's wonderful. Tom and Jenna Mori— thanks for talking with us.

TOM AND JENNA: Our pleasure. Thank *you*!

MARIA: OK, next, I'm going to talk to the kids! Don't go away!

page 169, Make Inferences

Example

MARK: Anyway, at some point, we just decided that we couldn't take care of Tonia and a new baby.

Excerpt One

MARION: . . . when we had Tonia, our daughter, I was thirty-eight. Tonia is so wonderful, and we love her more than anything. But . . . well, it isn't easy to raise a young child at our age.

MARK: That's for sure. We're always tired!

Excerpt Two

MARION: Um . . . I don't think so, because we spend a *lot* of time with her, and she has lots of friends.

MARK: That's for sure! She's very popular!

MARIA: Really! You know, that's interesting because I read that only children are often more popular—and also more intelligent—than children with siblings.

MARK: Yes, that IS interesting!

MARIA: Isn't it? It's really something to think about.

Excerpt Three

JENNA: Well, *before* we had a child, money wasn't really so important to us.

MARIA: That's interesting . . .

JENNA: But now . . . well, when you have a child, it's *different*. We want our son Jay to have a good life—you know—to go to a good school, take piano lessons, travel . . . And those things are very expensive!

Listening Two, page 171, Comprehension

MARIA SANCHEZ: Hello, and welcome back. So, what do kids think about being an only child? Let's find out right now! I'm going to speak to Marion and Mark's daughter, Tonia, and to Tom and Jenna's son, Jay. Hi, Tonia.

TONIA: [*Softly, shy*] Hi.

MARIA: How old are you, sweetheart?

TONIA: Eight.

MARIA: Eight. And Jay, you are . . . ?

JAY: I'm twelve.

MARIA: OK. Now Tonia, you're the only child in your family, right?

TONIA: Uh-huh.

MARIA: And is that OK with you?

TONIA: [*Defiantly*] No! I hate it . . .

AUDIENCE: [*Laughter*]

MARIA: Really . . . Why?

TONIA: Because I want a sister.

AUDIENCE: [*Stronger laughter*]

TONIA: All my friends have brothers and sisters. I'm the only kid in my class who doesn't have one!

MARIA: Oh, I see . . . Umm . . . did you ever talk to your parents about it?

TONIA: [*Sadly*] Yeah, I talked to my mom.

MARIA: And what did she say?

TONIA: She said, "I am so busy with you and with my job. We are not going to **have** another child."

MARIA: And how did you feel then?

TONIA: I was sad.

MARIA: But can you understand your parents' **decision**?

TONIA: [*Sounding resigned*] Yeah . . .

MARIA: Well, that's good.

TONIA: [*Defiantly*] But I still want a sister!

AUDIENCE: [*Laughter*]

MARIA: [*Laughing*] Well, here's a little girl who knows what she wants! Thank you, Tonia.

AND Jay, how about you? Do you feel the same way?

JAY: No, not at all. I like my family this way.

MARIA: Mmmm . . . But do you ever feel **lonely**?

JAY: No, I never feel **lonely**. I feel . . . special! My parents do a lot of things with me, and we always **have fun** together. And they also give me a lot of **opportunities** that kids in some big families don't have.

MARIA: What kinds of **opportunities**?

JAY: Well, the best thing is that we travel a lot, all over the world. Like, last summer, we went to Asia for a month. And this winter, we're going to go skiing in Europe.

MARIA: Wow, that's exciting!

JAY: Yeah, and I think we can do all of these things because it's just the three of us.
MARIA: You mean, because your parents **can afford** it?
JAY: Yeah, uh-huh . . .
MARIA: But do you ever feel different from your friends?
JAY: Mmmm . . . no, not in a bad way. I mean, every family is different, right?
MARIA: Yes, that's true.
JAY: So maybe I'm a little different because I enjoy doing things **alone**.
MARIA: That IS a little unusual for someone your age.
JAY: Well, my parents taught me how to enjoy doing things by myself. I don't **act** like a baby and cry because I don't have a **sibling** to do things with.
MARIA: What a **mature** young man you are!
JAY: Thank you.
MARIA: Thank you, Jay, and thanks to you, too, Tonia.
TONIA AND JAY: You're welcome.
MARIA: Well, there you have it—two children, and two very different opinions about being an only child. Thanks for watching!

page 173, Listening Skill

Example

MARIA SANCHEZ: Hello, and welcome back. So, what do kids think about being an only child? Let's find out right now! I'm going to speak to Marion and Mark's daughter, Tonia, and to Tom and Jenna's son, Jay. Hi, Tonia.
TONIA: [*Softly, shy*] Hi.
MARIA: How old are you, sweetheart?
TONIA: Eight.
MARIA: Eight. And Jay, you are…?
JAY: I'm twelve.
MARIA: OK. Now Tonia, you're the only child in your family, right?
TONIA: Uh-huh.
MARIA: And is that OK with you?
TONIA: [*Defiantly*] No! I hate it…
AUDIENCE: [*Laughter*]
MARIA: Really…Why?
TONIA: Because I want a sister.
AUDIENCE: [*Stronger laughter*]

UNIT 8: Soccer: The Beautiful Game

Listening One, page 193, Preview

Gooool!
It's a goal!
Goooool!

JANE: That is the sound of soccer, the world's **favorite** sport. Of course, soccer is still not very popular in the U.S. But with the Internet and satellite TV, the world is getting smaller, and today, Americans can see that people all over the world really love this game! To understand why people outside the U.S. love soccer so much, we went to Paolinho's Pizza Restaurant in Minneapolis, Minnesota, to watch the first **match** of World Cup soccer.

page 193, Main Ideas

Gooool!
It's a goal!
Goooool!
JANE: That is the sound of soccer, the world's **favorite** sport. Of course, soccer is still not very popular in the U.S. But with the Internet and satellite TV, the world is getting smaller, and today, Americans can see that people all over the world really love this game! To understand why people outside the U.S. love soccer so much, we went to Paolinho's Pizza Restaurant in Minneapolis, Minnesota, to watch the first **match** of World Cup soccer.
JANE: Hello. What is your name, and where are you from?
GILBERTO: I'm Gilberto, and I am from Brazil.
JANE: Why do you like soccer, Gilberto?
GILBERTO: Why? Ha! That is not even a question in Brazil. Soccer is our life. It is an art. It's like music— Does anyone ever ask you, "Why do you like music?"
JANE: Well, no . . .
GILBERTO: [*With enthusiasm*] Well, soccer is the same. You know, Pele, the famous Brazilian soccer player?
JANE: Sure, he . . .
GILBERTO: He called soccer "The Beautiful Game." Why? Because when the ball flies through the air, it's beautiful, and when the player jumps into the air, it's like he's flying—like a bird or a dancer. And when he heads the ball or **kicks** it across the **field** into the goal, it is **simple** and beautiful. It is perfect. It is like a . . .
JANE: [*Interrupting*] Thank you, Gilberto. And what about you, sir? What's your name and where are you from?
ERNESTO: I'm Ernesto from Mexico City.
JANE: And why do you like soccer, Ernesto?
ERNESTO: I don't LIKE soccer—I LOVE soccer! And look at all these people here—they all love it, too.
JANE: Yes, but why?
ERNESTO: Because soccer is like an international language. I come here to watch soccer with these soccer **fans** from all over the world. For example, I don't know this guy's name here—What's your name?

ANDERS: Anders.

ERNESTO: Yes, Anders—he's from Germany. And I don't really know him, but today we both want the **team** from Italy to **win**. You see, I'm Mexican, he's German, but we both love soccer. It's like there are really only two countries: the country that loves soccer and the country that doesn't understand.

ANDERS: [*Laughing*] That's the United States—the country that doesn't understand!

JANE: Well, we're trying! That's why I'm talking to you today! Anders, Ernesto said you're from Germany?

ANDERS: Yes, and this is my girlfriend, Marta. She's from Spain.

JANE: Hi, Marta.

MARTA: Hello.

JANE: What do you like about soccer?

ANDERS: Soccer is a sport for *everyone*. You don't need a lot of special things to play it—you just need a ball and a goal. It's **simple**. So everyone can play soccer.

MARTA: Yes, and also, everyone can understand soccer—not like American football. You have to read books to understand all of the **rules** in American football! Soccer is *simpler*—and it's also *more exciting* to watch.

JANE: So there are a few reasons that people love soccer. If you still don't understand, go and watch a **match** at a restaurant like Paolinho's. You might become a **fan**! With *The Sports File*, this is Jane Tuttle.

page 195, Make Inferences

Example

JANE: Why do you like soccer, Gilberto?

GILBERTO: Why? Ha! That is not even a question in Brazil. Soccer is our life. It is an art. It's like music— Does anyone ever ask you, "Why do you like music?"

Excerpt One

GILBERTO: You know, Pele, the famous Brazilian soccer player?

JANE: Sure, he . . .

GILBERTO: He called soccer "The Beautiful Game." Why? Because when the ball flies through the air, it's beautiful, and when the player jumps into the air, it's like he's flying—like a bird or a dancer.

Excerpt Two

JANE: And why do you like soccer, Ernesto?

ERNESTO: I don't LIKE soccer—I LOVE soccer! And look at all these people here—they all love it too.

JANE: Yes, but why?

ERNESTO: Because soccer is like an international language. I come here to watch soccer with these soccer fans from all over the world.

Excerpt Three

MARTA: Yes, and also, everyone can understand soccer—not like American football. You have to read books to understand all of the rules in American football!

Listening Two, page 197, Comprehension

COMMENTATOR: Welcome to "America Talks." This morning, we're taking calls from sports fans to hear your opinions about soccer: Why isn't soccer more popular in the United States? During the last World Cup, 700 million people all over the world watched the final match on television. 700 million! But many Americans, even big sports fans, did not even know that the World Cup was happening. How can Americans NOT be interested in a sport that the rest of the world loves—a sport that is so international? Our first caller is Bob from Kearny, New Jersey. Welcome to the show, Bob.

BOB: Hi. Thanks for taking my call.

COMMENTATOR: Bob, why isn't soccer popular in this country?

BOB: Well, I think it's mostly **because of** the **low scores**.

COMMENTATOR: Uh-huh . . .

BOB: You can have a great soccer match, but the final **score** can be 0 to 1. I think Americans like sports with *higher* scores.

COMMENTATOR: Interesting. And speaking of scores, people also say that **ties** are a problem for sports fans in the U.S. Americans really like one team to win and one team to **lose**.

BOB: Yeah, that's definitely another reason that soccer isn't very popular here.

COMMENTATOR: Thanks for the call, Bob. Next, we have Linda from Rochester, New York on the line. Hello, Linda.

LINDA: Hi. I think soccer is *less popular* here **because** we just didn't grow up with it. We didn't play it very much as kids, and there were no professional soccer teams, so we couldn't watch it on TV. Baseball and basketball were definitely more popular. And football.

COMMENTATOR: So you think the problem is just that soccer is not a traditional sport in this country?

LINDA: Yeah. Our traditional sports in the U.S. are baseball, football, and basketball. And if you watch all three of those sports, you're pretty busy. We don't really need another sport.

COMMENTATOR: Thanks for your comments, Linda. We have one more call, from Drew in Seattle, Washington. Drew, why do you think soccer isn't more popular here in the U.S.?

DREW: [*Older man*] Hi. I think **the reason** is that Americans love superstars. But we haven't had any really big American soccer stars yet. I mean, Pele played in the U.S. in 1975, but he's from Brazil, and that was a really long time ago. I think David Beckham made Americans more interested in soccer. He WAS a superstar, and so was his wife, Victoria. I think they helped soccer in the U.S. a lot.

COMMENTATOR: Yes, I agree.

DREW: But they're from England. If you ask me, we need an American superstar—someone like Michael Jordan. Then soccer will become more popular, for sure!

COMMENTATOR: OK, thanks for your call, Drew. And that's it for today's show. Tune in again tomorrow for *America Talks*.

page 198, Listening Skill

Example

BOB: Hi. Thanks for taking my call.

COMMENTATOR: Bob, why isn't soccer popular in this country?

BOB: Well, I think it's mostly **because** of the **low score**s.

COMMENTATOR: Uh-huh.

Excerpt One

COMMENTATOR: Interesting. And speaking of scores, people also say that ties are a problem for sports fans in the U.S. Americans really like one team to win and one team to lose.

BOB: Yeah, **that's definitely another reason** that soccer isn't very popular here.

Excerpt Two

LINDA: Hi. I think soccer is less popular here **because** we just didn't grow up with it. We didn't play it very much as kids, and there were no professional soccer teams, so we couldn't watch it on TV.

Excerpt Three

DREW: Hi. I think **the reason is tha**t Americans love superstars. But we haven't had any really big American soccer stars yet.

TEXT CREDITS

PHOTO CREDITS

THE PHONETIC ALPHABET

Consonant Symbols			
/b/	be	/t/	to
/d/	do	/v/	van
/f/	father	/w/	will
/g/	get	/y/	yes
/h/	he	/z/	zoo, busy
/k/	keep, can	/θ/	thanks
/l/	let	/ð/	then
/m/	may	/ʃ/	she
/n/	no	/ʒ/	vision, Asia
/p/	pen	/tʃ/	child
/r/	rain	/dʒ/	join
/s/	so, circle	/ŋ/	long

Vowel Symbols			
/ɑ/	far, hot	/iy/	we, mean, feet
/ɛ/	met, said	/ey/	day, late, rain
/ɔ/	tall, bought	/ow/	go, low, coat
/ə/	son, under	/uw/	too, blue
/æ/	cat	/ay/	time, buy
/ɪ/	ship	/aw/	house, now
/ʊ/	good, could, put	/oy/	boy, coin